HISTORY AND ARCHAEOLOGY OF GUJARAT THROUGH THE PRISM OF SKANDAPURĀṆA

About the Authors

Dr. S.C. Mishra taught History to undergraduate and postgraduate students at Delhi University for more than four decades. His most valuable contribution is a book, *The Evolution of Kauṭilya's Arthaśāstra: An Inscriptional Approach.* Besides, plethora of his research papers are published in reputed journals, edited books, proceedings of Indian History Congress and Magazines. His research interests include: Ancient World, Ancient Indian History and Literature, Archaeology, Numismatics and Epigraphy.

Dr. Manisha S. Agnihotri is a Professor of History at Janki Devi Memorial College, University of Delhi. She has contributed papers to the Indian History Congress, UGC Care listed Journals, edited books/volumes and a chapter in the textbook on European History published by Delhi University. Her research interests include: Medieval Indian History, Religious Thoughts and Practices in Early Medieval and Medieval India, Gender and Trans-Gender studies, and various ancient Indian literary and archaeological issues.

HISTORY AND ARCHAEOLOGY OF GUJARAT THROUGH THE PRISM OF SKANDAPURĀṆA

S. C. Mishra
Manisha S. Agnihotri

CONCEPT PUBLISHING COMPANY PVT. LTD.
NEW DELHI - 110 059

ISBN: 978-93-5594-623-2

First Published 2023

Published and Printed by

Since 1974

Concept Publishing Company Pvt. Ltd.
A/15-16, Commercial Block, Mohan Garden
New Delhi-110059 (India)
T : +91-11-41101460
E: publishing@conceptpub.com, *W*: www.conceptpub.com

Cataloging in Publication--Courtesy: D.K. Agencies (P) Ltd. <docinfo@dkagencies.com>

Mishra, S. C. (Suresh Chandra), 1949- **author.**
History and archaeology of Gujarat through the prism of Skandapurāṇa / S.C. Mishra, Manisha S. Agnihotri.
pages cm
Includes bibliographical references and index.
ISBN 9789355946232

1. Puranas. Skandapurāṇa. Brāhmakhaṇḍa. Dharmāraṇya māhātmya--Criticism, interpretation, etc. 2. Gujarat (India)--Civilisation. 3. Gujarat (India)--Antiquities. I. Agnihotri, Manisha S., author. II. Title.

LCC DS485.G8M57 2023 | DDC 954.75 23

Preface

We are really pleased to place this book before students, researchers, teachers, specialists and lay readers in general interested in Ancient (Indian) History, Archaeology and the Culture of Gujarat. Essentially, this is culmination of a research paper initially presented to the World Archaeological Congress Session–3, held at New Delhi in 1994 by the first co-author of this project. But later our joint venture and efforts have succeeded in the fruition of this work.

The present study locates and unravels the history and Archaeology of the settlement, decadence, rehabilitations of a place many a times in succession at different points of times in its long history as described in the Dharmāraṇya sub-section of the *Skandapurāṇa.* In spite of the fact that the anecdotes and accounts it describes, happen to be a blend of myths, legends and history, the enormous data it furnishes is quite useful for knowing the social, material and religious history of the area and its people under discussion. Therefore, in order to know the occurrence of successive developments at the sites and its influence zones during the time limits of our study, we have chosen to set the agenda by identifying and analysing the whole discourse, so to say, through the medium of the "Archaeological stratification of the text", itself, as it very often lays down threadbare the multifarious coeval developments both in the text and also on the archaeological sites at their respective spots.

But before this study is undertaken in detail, it is deemed necessary to identify the exact location of the site, or area of Dharmāraṇya on the basis of the descriptions of its landscapes, physiography, ecology, flora and fauna, the beginning of the human habitations and demography, because as will be seen in the discussions to follow, we come across the names of

Dharmāraṇya multiple times located in various other areas also mentioned in literary texts. Also for a clear comprehension of the beginning of the earliest settlements and the series and sequence of successive developments at the site, a gist of the narrative deemed necessary is given at the outset. Among other foci of the present study as depicted in the document are the identifications of the fifty five villages granted to the original Vāḍava settlers – Trivedi Brahmanas and Nineteen other villages of the subsequent breakaway group of the Chaturvedi Brahmanas. Further, this is also an endeavour to locate and know about the other 144 villages granted to the Brahmanas at a later time. Since some of the granted villages enumerated in the document have now grown into big cities, we have undertaken to examine the role played by various productive forces and also the relations of productions in the process of urbanisation of some of them like Vadodara, Godhra, Ahmedabad, Sitapur and others. As the document gives a vivid and fascinating accounts of various locations, dimensions, expansions and at times of shrinkages, or rupture of the area or centres and throws light on the religious and secular structures, this also has formed another aspects of our study. As the culture and material culture and the dynamics of their internal relations hold key to the proper understanding of the total history and archaeology of the contemporary society we have striven to bring out characteristic features of the nature of resemblances and divergences between the two sources – documentary and archaeological by forging reconciliation as pleaded by D.P. Dymond in his *Archaeology and History : A Plea for Reconciliation* (London, 1974). Various groups of religious sectaries, their marks and the formations of new and old professional groups both have been in the centre of our evaluation.

As our study progresses along the lines of agenda focusing on the stratification of the text of *Dharmāraṇya Māhātmya*, we have tried to examine and correlate the structural changes and developments stratawise at the sites. Since the entire document of *Dharmāraṇya Māhātmya* presents a picture of human habitations and their activities interspersed into all the four Indian Traditional Ages called *Kṛtayuga*, *Tretā*, *Dvāpara* and *Kaliyuga*, we have without any deviation treated them as a paradigm of four different cultural periods, phases or stratification of the text as it is. It is remarkable to note that each one of the four traditional ages of India as described in the text present a linear view of time instead of cyclical one, which is set to repeat time and again. On close examination at the time of stratification of the text, these four cultural periods have gone to extend up to ten sub-periods, or structural periods. Thus, these four cultural periods and ten structural periods have gone to subsume and display the entire data of the text for analysis and interpretations.

In the light of the fact that much of our study progresses along the old and Puranic genre of descriptions and interpretations, it may not be out of place to mention that the Vedic and Puranic texts were transmitted in the past in different ways by the priestly families. Puranic records were meant to contain, among other things, independent records of royal dynasties (*rājavaṁśānucharita*). These were recast by narrators and listeners, thereby losing much of their sheen and credibility. So far as the old Vedic records are concerned, these have been compared as if they were old gramophones which have preserved original recording. The Purāṇas with their contents on the other hand have been compared with an audio cassette, which has been dubbed and redubbed so many times that it is not an easy task to separate the original 'signal' from the accumulated noise. This dictum may hold good for the *Dharmāraṇya* sub-section of the *Skandapurāṇa*. If one looks at the transmission of the *Dharmāraṇya Māḥātmya* one finds this document to have been finally recited by Sūta to the gathering of sages (*Munis*) at Nimiṣa (Naimiṣāraṇya) in front of Śaunaka, the Chancellor after the conclusion of the twelve years *sattra*. Originally, it was recited by Vyāsa to Yama/ Dharma. Yama or Dharma recited it to Nārada and Nārada recited it to Yudhiṣṭhira, who narrated it to Vyāsa, the son of Satyawati in the middle of Kali and Dvāpara and finally, it was narrated to Sūta by Vyāsa who narrated it to the vast gathering of sages at Naimiṣāraṇya. One can easily comprehend that the stages of narration presented occasions for the addition or shrinkage of the text.

It is also said that Puranic history is not bunk, it is the geography that is misplace(d), that is why one comes across the transference of several place names at different far off places.

From here we move on to "culture". As much of our study revolves round culture(s) and history of the text as well as the archaeological data gathered from the sites, it becomes necessary to know about it. Today there are approximately one hundred definitions of "Culture". The fact is that the notion of culture is undergoing reconstruction. The rethinking about the notion of culture started from the 1960s onwards. In Anthropology, the term means shared by all members of a given society. If one speaks of culture "shared, then by whom? And in what ways?" This has got to be answered.

If we take a wider view of the subject, we come across several exponents of culture. We shall very briefly underline some major and prominent proponents, or schools of thought who have dealt with it in their respective ways. Among these mention may be made of D.D. Kosambi, Frankfurt School, Michel Foucault, Antonio Gramsci, Marxist scholars and post-Processualist scholars led by L.R. Binford and Ian Hodder. Very briefly, we shall sum up their views on culture. Most of them have made use of the metaphor of base and superstructure. D.D. Kosambi says, "Guess at the base from what remains of the superstructure". This may lead one to trace the unknown base through the known superstructure. The complete historical process through which social form has been reached is of prime importance. While recognising the autonomy of superstructure, Kosambi subscribed to the idea of superstructure reaching the base. There is dialectical relationship between base and superstructure with relative autonomy for the latter. The Frankfurt school thinkers too explained the relative autonomy of the superstructure, however, without overlooking homologous connections between culture and economic base. Foucauldian notion of discourse of culture is grounded in unequal relations and related to people and groups in different social positions. Antonio Gramsci too emphasised the necessary reciprocity between base and superstructure. There was emergence of some new Marxist historians, who heralded a departure from the productive force determinism of Marxist orthodoxy in base superstructure relations. Much of the post-Processualist view of culture is obviously borrowed from post-modernist trends in literature and the resonance of such trends in socio-cultural anthropology. Binford and Ian Hodder as the patrons of new and post-processualist archaeology are of continuing interests to historians and philosophers of Archaeology.

If we look into their views closely, we notice that most of them like D.D. Kosambi, Frankfurt school thinkers M. Foucault, Antonio Gramsci and the new genre of Marxist historians have given due weightage to the metaphor of base and superstructure relations and have granted superstructure relative autonomy. The cultural data amassed from the document called *Dharmāraṇya Māhātmya* and also from archaeological excavations has been tested through these models to observe and pinpoint continuity and changes in cultural assemblages to different phases and structural periods.

Having discussed the dialectics of base superstructure relations of culture, we now turn to the criss-cross placement and collation of the assemblage of cultural data obtained from the different strata of the archaeological sites by bringing them face to face with the delineated culture and material culture as expounded or extracted from the narrative of the document called *Dharmāraṇya Māhātmya* of the *Skandapurāṇa* through the medium of its archaeological stratification. It would be really very fruitful and justifiable in upholding the hypothesis of the archaeological stratification of the *Dharmāraṇya Māhātmya* text as it studies the narrated cultural data and structures chronologically, sequence and layerwise and also as expanded on a larger surface of the area of human habitation as delineated in the document compared to the data obtained from the (vertically) excavated sites of a limited area.

It may be pointed out that the textual description of the cultural assemblage, or material cultures at the focused sites and their area of dimensions starts from the lowest strata, which penetrated at the level of the oldest culture with the revelations of structures of the same time. This is followed by the newer phase of culture (deposited) in the next strata, covering almost the entire span of the narrated cultural materials scattered or present at the delineated sites. It is in this way that the textual description passing through other strata and extended zone reaches on to the uppermost level (unless of course, the layers are not disturbed), which is really the most recent level and gives and yields the contemporary materials at the site.

Thus in the ultimate recapitulation, it can be said that the textual narrative as it gradually ascends upwards from the deepest level of human habitation, it provides a panorama of total culture and history of that phase of narrative. It is always useful to know the cultural sequence of the site, besides covering a larger area as an exposure of culture of that time, which is usually not available on an excavated site.

The excavated sites, by and large, give only a limited cultural data from different sequence of the site spread in a smaller area, on account of its being a vertically excavated site. Generally, the horizontal excavations have been conducted on a very few sites. Therefore, they cannot present the holistic view of the culture of the area useful for historical reconstruction. Many important structures and remains of the time spread and scattered over a long range of distance remain untraced.

Seen from both the above angles of documentary narrative, covering a larger dimension of area and preserving enormous age old data are more advantageous than the vertically excavated sites, which have their limitations.

Thus, it is when we make use of both ways of studying a site that we stand better chances of retrieving corroborative and comparative view of our pasts. It is satisfying to note that the present study has made full use of this method very meticulously. It is hoped that similar studies would blaze further trails for research and findings of the past. The Maps and *Appendices* given towards the end will further illustrate and illuminate the discourse for the readers.

S.C. Mishra
Manisha S. Agnihotri

Acknowledgements

In completing the task of writing this book we are indebted to a large number of individuals, scholars and institutions. In the long list, the first and the foremost sense of indebtedness to be expressed is to Indian Council of Historical Research for its financial assistance in initial stage. We are also thankful to the authors for consulting and making use of their works, especially the maps and figures for illustration and elucidation in this book. Our thanks are also due to Dr. Praveen Kumar Mishra, Cartographic Assistant (Miranda House, Delhi University), for making the Maps for the book.

Concept, our publisher, has been a tremendous support. We are indebted to innumerable library personnel, especially those of Central Reference Library (Arts Faculty) in University of Delhi, the Archaeological Survey of India Library (ASI), Central Archaeological Library (Delhi), the ICHR Library, Indira Gandhi National Centre for the Arts (IGNCA) library and many others.

In the end we express our heart-felt gratitude to our family and friends for their encouragement and support. Discussions with them on various issues proved very beneficial to us. Without their constant support, encouragement and help the presentation of this work could not have been possible.

While we are extremely grateful to all the individuals mentioned here, the responsibility for the views expressed and the faults, rests entirely with us alone.

S.C. Mishra
Manisha S. Agnihotri

Roman Equivalents of Nāgārī Letters

अ	a	क्	k	ढ्	ḍh	र्	r
आ	ā	ख्	kh	ण्	ṇ	ल्	l
इ	i	ग्	g	त्	t	व्	v
ई	ī	घ्	gh	थ्	th	श्	ś
उ	u	ङ्	ṅ	द्	d	ष्	ṣ
ऊ	ū	च्	ch	ध्	dh	स्	s
ए	e	छ्	chh	न्	n	ह्	h
ऐ	ai	ज्	j	प्	p	क्ष्	kṣ
ओ	o	झ्	jh	फ्	ph	त्र्	tṛ
औ	au	ञ्	ñ	ब्	b	ज्ञ्	jñ
अं	aṅ	ट्	t	भ्	bh	ढ़्	rh
अः	aḥ	ठ्	th	म्	m		
ऋ	ṛ	ड्	ḍ	य्	y		
लृ	ḷ						

Anusvāra (.) ṁ
Visarga (:) ḥ

Contents

PART - I

1
Gist of the Narratives of *Dharmāraṇya Māhātmya*

A. Gist of the Narratives of *Dharmāraṇya Māhātmya*

It is claimed in the Dharmāraṇya section of the Brahmakhaṇḍa of the *Skandapurāṇa* that Dharmāraṇya was repaired after its decadence and made to resettle with 18,000 departed Trivedi Brahmanas by Rāma after establishing Sitapur and other 55 villages made by him with all necessary provisions. The names of these 55 villages are mentioned four times in the text in one context or the other.[1] It is said that the grant of these 55 villages to the Trivedi Brahmanas was recorded on a copper plate charter written by Rāma himself giving details about his lineage, time and place and marking it with his own seal[2] in the Tretā Yuga at the second leg of his pilgrimage to the place which had been famous as Dharmāraṇya in Kṛtayuga, Satyamandira in Tretā, Vedabhavana in Dvāpara and Moheraka in Kaliyuga.[3] The 18,000 Trivedi Brahmanas along with their retinue are stated to have inhabited this place ever since its establishment by Kājesh, the three Gods in Kṛtayuga. Some of them continued to dwell there throughout iṇ four traditional ages on the strength of the said charter given by Rāma. But this settlement underwent several phases of decadence, resettlement and transformations at different points of time in its long history.

The entire 'Dharmāraṇya Māhātmya' in general, and its various legends in particular, assume considerable significance, for these shed light not only on the archaeo-historical aspects but also on several unknown facets of socio-religious developments taking place in the core area on the one hand, and the periphery and catchment areas of the settlement on the other. The Māhātmya talks of the settlement, intermittent desertions, decadence, re-occupations, outflow, desolateness, renovations/repairs, resettlement and expansion of the same place as many as ten times in succession in its chequered occupational history. Some dreadful demons like Jṛṁbhaka, Lohāsura, Lolajihvā, Karṇāta and Kumārapāla (King) appear to have been the prime movers in the enactment of the spectacular play of decadence and displacement of the 18,000 Trivedi Brahmanas with their 36,000 *Vanik* (merchant) retinue and more than 1,44,000 Śūdras, who had peopled this area. They took to burning, destroying, eloping with the newly wed couples, terrorizing, forfeiting and derecognizing the charter and suzerainty over the area under discussion, with the onset of Kaliyuga. Cropping up of differences in the customs, language and dress among the inhabitants, and intrusion of the *Mlechchhas* and Kolavidhavaṅsin, were the other causes of the decay. By and large, whenever there was some problem, the inhabitants of this place had taken to their heels in 'ten directions'. Twice, they are stated to have gone to other famous religious centres. Leaving the earth once, all the deities sought refuge in Naimiṣāraṇya.

The greatest setback to the settlement and to the Trivedi Brahmanas came in the Kaliyuga, when Kumārapāla, the king of Kanyakubja seized the donated villages of the Brahmanas and deprived them of subsistence. They temporarily left, but later, thanks to the help of Rāma's protege, Hanumāna, and the renewal of the charter they are stated to have recovered the area.

Later, kin-conflicts among the 18,000 Brahmanas for the rights over these villages and enjoyment of subsistence led to the formation of a splinter group of 15,000 Chaturvedis, who were made to settle at a place called Sukhavasanapur on the outskirts of Dharmāraṇya. They were spread over 19 villages.[4]

The whole of the foregoing account cannot be accepted literally *in toto*, for it seems to represent a later attempt around, or after A.D. 1200 for propagation of Vaiṣṇavism in Gujarat by the Audīchya Brahmanas, who migrated there. However, it may be useful to study the archaeology and history of the places with which the Brahmanas and merchants were associated; these places also include Vadodara and Godhra.

The present study primarily aims at the identification of the 55 villages granted to the Brahmanas and 19 other villages of the breakaway group of the Chaturvedis. Since, a large number of these villages have become big cities, we propose to examine the role played by the productive forces in the process of urbanisation of some of them like Vadodara, Godhra, Ahmedabad, Sitapur and others. The text gives a vivid account of the location, extent of the area, and various religious and secular structures. It also describes the settlements and the groups of people of different persuasions and professions. We, therefore, propose to examine the material culture of these places, and check it with the details given in the text to see the nature of resemblance, if any, between the two. According to the Māhātmya, interspersed in the four traditional ages, the whole human occupation at Dharmāraṇya can be divided into four cultural periods, which can be subdivided into ten structural periods.

B. Transmission of the Text of 'Dharmāraṇya Māhātmya'

Before we further descend into textual details about the history of the settlements, it would be useful to trace the origin, value and method of the transmission of these legends. The legends can be taken to be a compendium of floating, or oral type of literature because of the method followed in the transmission of their accounts. First of all, it was told by Vyāsa to Yama/Dharma, who described it to Nārada. Later, Nārada narrated it to Yudhiṣṭhira in short, but Vyāsa, the son of Satyavati, narrated in detail, in the middle of the *Kali* and *Dvāpara*. Finally, listening from his teacher, Vyāsa, Sūta narrated it to a vast gathering of the hermits (*munis*) assembled at Naimiṣa, in front of Śaunaka, the Chancellor (*Kulapati*) in Nimiṣakṣetra after the conclusion of the twelve years sacrifice (*sattra*) held there.

The original transmitters of the oral traditions may have been the local religious priests and *pandits*, who composed and gathered the legends of the holy centres. Therefore, this type of text can neither be taken to be a fixed body of literature nor to be a homogeneous composition. Initially, an inventory of sacred information about the *tirthas*, local priests gave it definite shape. Eventually, it was redacted and included by the composer of the Brahmakhaṇḍa in the *Skandapurāṇa*.

Although, it is emphatically stated that Vyāsa narrated chronologically the past, present and future historical happenings of Dharmāraṇya[5] and some of the narratives of the text are said to be based on the short narratives (*ākhyāns*) and episodes of the past (*upākhyāns*), the two constituents of history writing of those times, there remains no doubt about the fact that myths, legends and history are mixed up in the narrative. Similarly, the references to the two dates given in the Māhātmya, if taken on their face value, push back the antiquity of these settlements to a period not less than 30,800 years back, past now. According to the Māhātmya, the earliest event took place three *ayuta* (30,000) years ago in *Tretā*. The second event refers to the happenings in the *Kali* age at the advent of Kumārapāla, the king of Kanyakubja, who can easily be assigned to a period between A.D. 1114-1173. Since the legends of the Māhātmya were narrated to Yudhiṣṭhira in the middle of the *Kali* and *Dvāpara* by Yama[6], this event should indicate the termination of the *Dvāpara* and coming of the *Kaliyuga*. As this coming is connected with Kumārapāla, it appears that the redaction of the legends and their assimilation into the Brahmakhaṇḍa must not have taken place earlier than the twelfth century.

NOTES

1. See the Consolidated List of Common Names of the 55 Villages Granted to Brahmanas (*Appendix I*). These names occur in four different places in contexts of the places, *gotras*, *pravaras* and the *gotra devis* of the Brahmanas.
2. *Tenedaṁ śāsanaṁ dattam akshayaṁ na kathaṁ bhavet*
   svavaṁśa varṇanaṁ tatra likhitvā svayameva tu
   deśa kālādikaṁ sarvaṁ lilekha vidhipūrvakam
   svamudrāchihnitaṁ tatra traividyebhyastathā dadau,
   Shriskandamahāpurāṇam, 3.2.34.15-17 (Re-edition of Kshemaraja Shri Kṛṣṇadāsa's edition, published from Shri Veṅkateshvara Steam Printing Press, Bombay : *The Skanda-Mahāpurāṇam III Part* : Shri Brāhmakhaṇḍa, by Nag Publishers, Delhi, 1986. Hereafter (*Skandapurāṇa*).
3. *Dharmāraṇyaṁ kṛtayuge tretāyām satyamaṅdiraṁ*
   dvāpare vedabhavanaṁ kalau moherakam smṛtaṁ,
   Skandapurāṇa, 3.2.40.67-68.
4. Śilā, Maṅḍorā, Evaḍī, Gundarāṇā, Kalyāṇīā, Degāmā, Nāyakapurā, Ḍaliā, Kaḍovyā, Kohāṭoyā, Haradīyā, Bhadukīyā, Saṁprāṇāvā, Kaṅdarāvā, Vasarovā, Śaraṇḍāvā, Lolāsaṇā, Varolā and Nāgalapurā, *Skandapurāṇa,* 3.2.39.78-82.
5. *Bhūtam bhāvyaṁ bhaviṣyaṁ cha uttamādhamamadhyamaḥ*
   vāchayiṣyati tatsarvamitihāsa samudbhavaṁ
   dharmāraṇyasya sakalaṁ vṛttaṁ yadyatpurātanaṁ
   vyāsaḥ satyavatīputro vadiṣyati cha teakhilaṁ, Skandapurāṇa, 3.2.1.108-109.
6. *Yamena kathitaṁ sarvam yachchhrutaṁ brahmasaṅsadi*
   ādimadhyāvasānam cha sarvam naivātra śaṁsayaḥ
   kalidvāparayor-madhyedharmaputramyudhiṣṭhiram, Skandapurāṇa, 3.2.1.76-77.

2
Archaeological Stratification of the Text of *Dharmāraṇya Māhātmya*

CULTURAL PERIOD I

A. Structural Period I

The four traditional divisions of time help us to visualize and understand the sequence of events from the viewpoints of the narrator and redactor of the text. Coming to the details, the first cultural period of Noheraka (*sic*) (for Moheraka) is marked by two breaks in the occupation of the site. It has three structural periods. After the end of the second break, we see the extension and expansion of the site. After the first break, which takes 100 years later, we get the addition of 36,000 *vanijas* to the population of the site. So far as the nature of the soil in this area is concerned, it is said that all the *tirthas* at Dharmāraṇya are saline, or unfertile land (*ūṣara*). It is adorned by Brahmā, Viṣṇu and Ṃaheśa, the world protectors (*lokapālaiḥ*), protectors of directions (*dikpālaiḥ*), divine mothers, who are seven in numbers (*mātṛbhiḥ)*, fifty forms of the *śaktis* of Śiva (*śivaśaktibhiḥ*), sky gods, perhaps twenty seven in numbers (*gaṇdharvaiḥ*), divine nymphs, the wives of Gaṇdharvas (*apsarobhiḥ*), the people engaged in oblation (*Yajñakarmabhiḥ*), spirits (*bhūta*), demons (*vetāla*), a female demon attendant on Durgā (*Sākinī*), a female imp attending on Kali (*ḍākini*), deities of the planets (*grahadevaiḥ),* tutelary deities (*adhidevataiḥ)* and the gods and demons (*surāsuraiḥ*). It was graced by a large number of sacrifices (*yajñaiḥ*) and excellent sages (*munis*), lions, tigers, elephants, birds, cows, buffaloes, horses, deers, boars and various types of wild beasts. Initially, it was a seat of the king. The place is important for giving balls of rice to the deceased ancestors (*pinḍadāna*). This place is also marked by the performance of the horse sacrifice (*aśvamedha*). It was established by Kājesh by bringing 18,000 Vāḍavas from various countries.[1] Many cottages of the sages were made for their living. The Vāḍavas, who settled here, had twenty-four remote ancestors (*gotra*) and twenty-four eminent ancestors (*pravara*). As regards the physical features of the Vāḍavas, they had many small hairs (*romabhiḥ*) on their bodies and were black in complexion. In order to remove fear from the ghosts (*yakṣa*), demons (*piśācha*), especially from Jṛṁbhaka, the Yakṣa, holy men (*siddha*), tutelary deities (*varayoginī*) and Śrimātā were established for their welfare. One tutelary deity (*yoginī*) was set up for each remote ancestor (*gotra*).The female deity (*śakti*), who was capable of protecting a *gotra*, became its family deity (*kuladevī*). In this way, twenty-four female deities (*gotradevī*), e.g. Śrimātā, Tāriṇī, Devī, Asāpurī, Gotrapā, Ichchhā, Ārtināsini, Pippalā, Vikāravasā, Jaganmātā, Mahāmātā, Siddhā, Bhaṭṭārikā, Kadambā, Vikarā, Mīthā, Suparṇā, Vasujā, Mātaṇgī, Mukteshvarī, Bhadrā, Mahāśakti, Mahābalā, Chāmuṇḍā and Mahādevi were established by the trinity for the worship of the Brahmanas.

There seems to be some problem with the settler Vāḍavas, as after 100 years, on the visit of the three gods, who had gone to take stock of the situation, the Brahmanas had gone in 'ten directions'. However, they were not impelled by any fear, but did so in order to bring flowers, grass and other things, after leaving their cottages. To save them from this exertion, 36,000 strong merchants (*vaṇija*) were created by Kāmadhenu at the behest of the three deities. Each Brahman got two *vaṇik* attendants. These *vaṇijas* took the *gotras* of those Brahmanas. They and their sons were created to be the slaves/attendants of the Brahmanas. As regards the religious leanings of these Brahmanas, they belonged to different sects. Some of them were the followers of Vaiṣṇavism, others were Śaivites and still others followed Yama. Those who practised sacrifice (*yājakāḥ*) performed sacrifice (*yajña*) and made oblation to fire (*agnihotra*). The Vaiśyas provided the Brahmanas with food, water, flower and fruits. Their wives did the winnowing, making of fuels from cow-dung, and other household chores for the Vāḍavas. An altar, eight miles in extent, was raised for the Brahmanas. After doing sacrifices (*yajña*) for 100 years, they are stated to have got rid of the demons (*daitya*).

On the basis of this description, nothing serious seems to have happened, but, as will be seen, the fleeing of the Brahmanas in 'ten directions', is figuratively used throughout the text to denote desertion and decay. It seems that the settlement decayed after 100 years of its origin. With the addition of a population of 36,000 Vaiśyas, with their wives and children, the area of the settlement seems to have expanded and the second structural period begun.

B. Structural Period II

I. *Expansion, Migrations and Desertions*

It seems that the order restored on the site was not to last long, because in the Kṛta era, itself (*tatah kālena mahatā kṛtākhya yuga paryaye*), after the passage of a long period, Lohāsura[2], the prime mover of destruction, came on the scene, started penalising the Śūdras and *Vaṇijas*, teasing the Brahmanas and destroying their altars. Ruined by Lohāsura, the Vāḍavas left that place with their families and went in 'ten directions'.[3] Some of the Śūdras, Brahmanas and Vaiśyas went together to Muktāraṇya, a place not far off from that place and founded settlements. They established a place called Vajiṅgrāma. Śaṁbhugrāma was settled by Śaṁbhu *vaṇija*. Some of the *vaṇijas* were destroyed due to fear. They had settled a village called Maṇḍala grāma, not much away from that place. Aḍālaja village was settled by those merchants, who reached there from different paths. Since then, the villages came to be known after the name of the resident merchants of the village. Due to their displacement, *Vaṇijas* and Brahmanas stayed away from

Dharmāraṇya. As they were afraid and illusioned, they came to be known as Moha. Having accomplished his task, Lohāsura went back to his place, only to further bring havoc to the site, later. Thus, it is clear from the above description that the nucleus of the settlement was expanded in the directions of the villages named above.

II. *The Second Expansion*

The second phase of expansion of the settlement in the first cultural period is in the area of Śivakṣetra, where Sarasvati, which owed its origin to Surekhādrau, flowed. There are many religious sites located in this area. Govatsa *tīrtha*, which was visited by Mārakaṇḍeya, lay near Dvārāvatī in the form of Svayaṁbhuva liṅga. The king, Bahulārka, who was a great devotee of Śiva established Govatsa liṅga. Another religious site, called Chaṇḍāla, was established in front of Devālaya. There are many other places of religious significance near Govatsa *tīrtha*. Sarasvati, Śivakṣetra, Gaṅgā and Gaṅgā kūpa, these are located at a place, where two elephants are standing. In the south-west direction (*nairta*) of Govatsa, is an iron pillar (*lohayaṣṭikā*). Rudra himself is said to be standing there in the form of Svayaṁbhuva liṅga. At Lohayaṣṭi, *Śrāddha* is performed, after bathing at Sarasvati. There is Mokṣa *tirtha* on the bank of Sarasvati, where penance is done. At Rudra *tirtha*, people make the gift of cows (*godāna*), and gold is given in donation at Viṣṇu *tīrtha*.

CULTURAL PERIOD II

A. Structural Period III

The second cultural period, which according to the Māhātmya, began 30,800 years ago in *Tretā yuga*, shows four structural periods, the same numbers of desertions and expansions and migrations twice. On account of distinct landmarks, the area is easily identifiable and seems to be materially rich.

I. *Extent of the Nuclear Zone*

In the third structural period of the second cultural phase, desolateness of the nuclear area seems to have continued, but we come across certain landmarks, which are useful for identification. According to the Māhātmya, the area is spread over several *yojanas*. At one place it says that its extent was eight miles. The forest of Dharmāraṇya was covered with the wood-apple trees, called *Bel* (*vilva*), the plants of the Calotropis cetremonies called *madār* (*arka*), acacia catechu (*khadira*), the trees of Jonesia Asoka Roxb. (*aśoka*) and feronia elephantum (*kapittha*) trees, three *ayuta* (30,000) years ago in the Tretā yuga, while Yama was on penance. Although, the area was desolate, yet some cottages, fire places (*agnyāgāra*), Vardhamāna pond, near Indrasthāna, are said to have occupied it. Among other sites, the Viśveśvara liṅga, the Svayaṁbhuva liṅga, Bhūteśvara liṅga/Bhūtanath and other deities' liṅgas are prominent. It is believed that Bhūteśvara liṅga takes away all the diseases. By bathing at Dharmavāpī and visiting Dharmeśvara, man was absolved of all sins. *Śrāddha* was performed at Bhūteśvara. Dharmavāpī is located in the centre of Viśveśvara and Dharmeśvara, and this first *tīrtha* (*ādi tīrtha*) was graced by Kājesha, i.e. the three deities.

B. Structural Period IV

It is said that at the termination of the *yuga* (*yugānta kāle*) in the beginning of *Tretā*, the demon, Lolajihvā, having conquered many places, caused temporary setbacks to the site and the Brahmanas, by burning their towns. The resident Brahmanas went back as they had come. A duel between Lolajihvā and Śrīmātā ended the decay, as the demon was killed with the discus of Viṣṇu. Consequently, the Vāḍavas reoccupied the deserted place.[4]

I. *Landmarks of Satyamandira*

Further description of the text gives the landmarks of Satyamandira in the Ravikṣetra. In order to protect

Satyamandira, the city was established as before. In the East, there was Dharmeśvara, in the South Gaṇanāyaka/ Gaṇādhyakṣa, in the West, Bhānu and in the North Svayaṁbhuva. In the beginning, there was rampart (*prākāra*) with standards (*dhvajaiḥ*). There was also a place for Brahmanas called Brāhmaṇāyatana. In the middle was a platform (*pītha*) built of bricks and four broad ways (*pratolī*) with gates. In the southern *pratolī* there was single-toothed Gaṇādhyakṣa (*ekadantam gaṇādhyakṣa*) for the protection of the people. Towards the West of Śaṁbhu was located Kaśyapātmaja. That area was called Ravikṣetra. Aśvin deva was present there. Saṁjñā and/or Chhāyā Saṁjñā had their places. There were two deep water reservoirs (*kuṇḍa*) here. Another important reservoir considered sacred for bathing, was Ravi Kuṇḍa. Worship of Bakulārka was considered rewarding there.[5]

II. *Hayagrīva Viṣṇu*

Horse-mouthed Hari was stationed at Siddhasthāna. A pilgrimage centre called Mukteśa, or Mokṣeśvara Śaṁbhu was established by Viṣṇu. There, a deity's pond (*devasara*), bubbling with the waves of water, was considered very pious.

III. *Twelve Śaktis and Their Locations*

As before, twelve Śaktis were established in Satyamandira for the protection of its inhabitants. Śrīmātā was established at Madārikā and Śāntā at Nandāpur; Sāvitrī in the middle of the jungle. Jñānajā was established for killing demons. Among other tutelary deities Gāyatrī, Pakshiṇī, Devī, Pippalā, Āśāpurī are important. Chhatrajā was established towards the west of Dharmāraṇya. There was a tank in front of it. Anand was established earlier for the protection of the Brahmanas in the city of its own name. Towards the south was Śāntādevī (the eight handed goddess).

C. Structural Period V

Structural Period V witnessed the desertion of Satyamandira, migration of its people to big centres of pilgrimage and also expansion of the nuclear zone of its earlier settlements. The desertion took place, when a demon, Karṇāṭa terrified the Vaṇijas and Vāḍavas, and made them leave their places.[6] He caused obstructions in the smooth performances of vedic rites in all countries and villages. He burnt cities, and eloped with the newly wed couples. Due to this, the Brahmanas of that place fled in 'ten directions'. The lord of the earth (*bhūmidevāḥ*) deserted the place, and wherever there were big centres of pilgrimage, they went there.[7] In this way, Karṇāṭa teased the deniziens of this place. Mātā Mātaṅgī (eighteen armed goddess) stood by the side of the banyan tree. In the duel that ensued between the demon and Mātaṅgī, missile (*śataghnī*) was employed by the demon against the goddess. Śyāmalā, the sister of Mātaṅgī, is credited to have killed this demon at a place called Moṭeraka, yet he is said to have gone in the southern direction to found a country after his name. A mark with crescent, distinguished by a dot over it (◡̇) (*ardhabiṁbaka tilaka*) is prescribed to be put as a mark on the forehead by the Brahmanas.

I. *Dharākṣetra : The Abode of Twenty One Family Deities (Kuladevatas)*

Besides the sites of Mātaṅgī and Śyāmalā, there are other important places of religious significance. These are Indrasara and Indreśvara/Indratīrtha, Jayanteśa or Jayanta liṇga deity. Some Śaivite places are to be found in Dharākṣetra. Twenty-one family deities (*kuladevatas*), born from the body of Pārvatī find specific mention. These are Bhaṭṭārikā, Chhatrā, Ovikā, Jñānajā, Bhadrakālī, Maheśī, Simhorī, Dhanamarddanī, Gātrā, Śāntā, Śeṣadevī, Vārāhī, Bhadrayoginī, Yogeśvari, Mahālajjā, Kuleśi, Śakulāchitā, Tāraṇī, Vanakānandā, Chāmuṇḍā, Sureśvarī and Darabhaṭṭārikā.

II. *Śaktis and Residential Goddesses (Sthānavāsinī Devis)*

The tutelary goddesses were created at the time of the first settlement for the protection of the Brahmanas in all directions—Āśāpurī, Gātrāyī, Chhatrāyī, Jñānajā, Pippalāmbā, Śāntā,

Siddhā, Bhaṭṭārikā, Kadambā, Vikaṭā, Mīthā, Suparṇā, Vasujā, Mātaṅgī, Vārāhī, Mukteśvarī, Bhadrā, Mahāśakti, Simharā and Mahābalā.

III. *Extension of the Dharākṣetra Area*

As regards the places of the most important tutelary goddesses, some of them have been located. Towards the north of this place, near Āśāpūrna in the east, is Ānandā. Vasantī is in the north. In the south-western (*nairta*) direction is Śāntā. There is also Bhaṭṭarīdevi. Seven miles away from this place is Kṣemalābhā in the east direction. Towards the south, seven miles away from this place, is Vindhyavāsinī. In the west is Nimbajādevī. In the north corner at some distance is Suvarṇākṣā. Towards the north-west quarter (*vāyu-koṇa*), 2 miles away from that place is Kṣetradharā Mahādevī. One *krośa* away from the city towards the north is Karṇikā. In the south-western direction are the goddesses of water (*jalamātara*).

D. Structural Period VI

I. *Harikṣetra*

This structural period presents a spectacular picture of desolateness of the area, for a period of twelve years. In spite of the death of demon Lohāsura, the Brahmanas did not return to the site. In the beginning of the *Tretā* age, Rāma, who undertook the pilgrimage of this centre twice, is credited to have repaired the decay, donated 144 villages for the subsistence of the Brahmanas and provided them with 36,000 vaiśyas and 1,25,000 Māṇdalika Vaṇijas. Apart from settling the core area, there seems to be further expansion of the settlement towards the area known as Harikṣetra. During this phase, Rāma, obsessed with the idea of undertaking pilgrimage to absolve himself of the sins accruing due to the assassination of Brahmarākṣasas, came to Dharmāraṇya, followed by his retinue, with Vasiṣtha in the vanguard. After a ten days' journey, he is stated to have reached Dharmāraṇya *en route* Māṇḍalikapur, where he stayed for a night, with the inhabitant merchants. Riding a palanquin, he reached another place, known as Madhuvāsanakagrāma.[8]

II. *Establishment of Rāmeśa and Kāmeśvara on Survarṇā River*

In the land called Harikṣetra, Rāma looked for a land suitable for sacrifice (*yajña*) on the southern bank of the river Suvarṇā. He inspected the religious spots, sites and temples. There, he established Rāmeśa and Kāmeśvara on both the banks of the river Suvarṇā, in the north-west region (*vāyu*) of this place. In the midnight, he listened to the wailing of Śrīmātā, who narrated the story of the desolateness of the area for twelve years at a stretch[9], as the Brahmanas and the *Vaṇijas* had gone in 'ten directions', due to the fear of Lohāsura. That demon was killed, but due to his fear they were not going back.[10]

III. *Spectacles of Desolateness on the Eve of Rāma's Visit*

The text narrates vividly the following: The lakes, which used to be flooded with the people, about to bathe and donate, show only boars. The ponds which used to look beautiful due to the gracious presence of the excellent women couples, engrossed in amorous pastime, bears descend on them now. The places, which used to be strewn with abundance of excellent blossoms, are now covered with spiky trees, full of lions and tigers. The lands, which used to be the sporting grounds of the princes, now show cubs of tigers playing pleasantly. Where the Vāḍavas used to chant Vedas, now there appears the terrible howling of jackals. Where, there used to be seen smokes of sacrificial fire in every home, there, now could be seen smokes, even in forest which was engulfed in conflagration. Where dancers danced in front of the Brahmanas, now, spirits, demons and ghosts dance there, in infatuation. Where, kings used to sit in courts, engaged in counsel, on those places, are living Bos Gavaecus (ox), bears and porcupines. The places, which used to be the abode of Brahmanas and *vaṇijas*, show images, inlaid with small stones or mosaic (*kuṭṭima pratimā*) and caves (*bila*). Where, there were all-round cavities of trees (*koṭarāṇi*) are round windows (*gavākṣāṇi*). Where in olden days, the platforms (*chatuṣka*) of sacrificial altars (*yajña vedī*) were raised, today that can be seen surrounded by heaps of ant-hills (*valmīka nichayaiḥ*). This type of desolate place all-round, is my dwelling, which has become so due to the departure of *dvijas.*[11]

The 18,000 excellent Vāḍavas, who were proficient in the Vedas, came from sixty four *gotras*. The Vāḍavas graced the place, where the King Bakulārka, along with Saṁjñā, Kumāra Aśvin and Kubera were stationed and where, Śrīmātā, popularly known as Bhaṭṭārikā lived. These Brahmanas were of many varieties. Some lived on the gleanings of corn (*śiloñchhajīvikāḥ*), some had a single meal during the day (*ekāhikā*); some lived on unsolicited alms (*svāmṛtavṛttayaḥ*), others had grains stored in jars sufficient for one year's consumption (*kuṁbhīdhānyā*) and still others were engaged in six duties of Brahmanas—studying or repeating the Vedas, teaching it, offering sacrifices, conducting them for others and giving and accepting gifts. But, one thing that was common to them was that all of them had established Trimūrti (the image of three deities), in their respective houses.

When Śrīmātā appealed to him, Rāma agreed to bring back the said Brahmanas. He established this place and said that since Śrīmātā had spoken the truth, it would be known as the temple of truth, Satyamandira. After the valiant search operation by one lac retinue of Rāma, the Brahmanas were brought back. Rāma, with the instruction of Śrīmātā, promised to undertake the repair of the desolate place (*jīrṇoddhāra*)[12], which seems to have taken place at Harikṣetra near Dharmakūpa in Dharmāraṇya.[13]

IV. *Acts of Renovations and the Grant of 144 Villages Through Charter*

1. *Landmarks of Structures*

When the levelling operations of the mountains of ruins were over, outer halls (*bahiḥ śālā*), living houses (*gṛha śālā*) and Brahma's hall (*Brahma śālā*), adequately provided with household paraphernalia, riches, grains, and metals were raised, and then, they were handed over to the Traividya Brahmanas, with 144 villages for subsistence (*vetana*). The 36,000 *Vaṇijas*, who were called upon to serve the Brahmanas, were provided with a white chowry (fly whisk) and a sword each, with the instructions (from Rāma) that on auspicious and ceremonial occasions like, marriage, those should be worn by them[14] as Rāma's mark. Other *Vaṇijas,* 1,25,000 in numbers, engaged in trade at Māṇdalika, too, were given the insignia, double in numbers, i.e., two chowries and two swords each, with the same instructions. After this, places and spots of worship were established. Brahma, Śrīmātā, Śūnyasvāmī Hari, Gaṇa and many other deities were settled. We come across some secular structures also in the scheme of Rāma's undertakings. Besides building seven storied mansions (*saptabhaumika prāsāda*), many ponds for Gods (*deva vāpī*), Rāma, also built ramparts (*prākāra*), broad ways (*pratolī*), forts (*durga*), provided with various equipments and things of necessary use. Reservoirs (*kuṇḍa*), ponds (*sara*), tanks, wells, all were built in good numbers. On all auspicious, or ceremonial occasions, Bakulārka and Śrīmātā were offered shares (*bhāga*) for the unhindered success of a work. After the successful completion of these buildings in Dharmāraṇya, Trivedis were handed over the possession of them, with a copper plate written by Rāma himself, and entrusted the obligation of protecting the place and its inhabitats, to Hanumāna. The charter, in question, is said to have been written in accordance with the rules of law (*dharmaśāstra*) at a place, where Śūnyasvāmī and Bakulārka were situated; where the tutelary deity, Tāriṇī was submerged in the sea of the world. Why copper is indestructible? There is reason for that, "Rāma had numerous enumerated achievements to his credit, then why a charter (*śāsana*) written by him should not be indestructible". This is, what has been argued by the author of the Purāṇa, who himself raised this question. Rāma, the son of Daśaratha, who was 44 years of age, is stated to have written this charter himself, after worshipping Viṣṇu and giving necessary details about his lineage. By giving all details of time and place methodically, and marking it with his seal (*svamudrā chihnitaṁ*), gave it to the Trivedis.[15] In this wonderful charter of Rāma, it is heard that Rāma, after giving the land had asked the future Kings to honour and protect it in their respective rules. Since then, the copper plate charter became an object of worship for the Vāḍavas forever. They worshipped it with the red sandals, flowers, perfumes, gold and silver flowers. Everyday, they lit lamps, made of seven wicks in front of it, and gave offering of edibles (*naivedya*). The charter (*śāsana*) was given to the Brahmanas, with a view to allowing them to enjoy on its basis, the granted lands, as long as the Sun and Moon last. After this generous act, Rāma is stated to have gone back to Ayodhya, only to reappear again in the next period.

The procedures, reportedly followed in recording the grant of the villages till perpetuity on the copper plates, by fixing the seal of the donor (King), giving necessary details about his lineage, recording the time and place of the grants and issuing a clarion call to the current and future Kings to comply to the appeals of the donor to protect the grants—all these verily seem to be strikingly in conformity with the rules of the *Yājñavalkya Smṛti* mentioned in the Section of the Duties of the Kings (*Rājadharma Prakaraṇa*), where the law-giver has laid down the same rules and procedures for recording the grants of land by the donor with the instructions for the petty future lords of men to follow them without any deviation of the rules.[16]

CULTURAL PERIOD III

A. Structural Period VII

Surprisingly, at the second leg of Rāma's pilgrimage to the above settlement, previously called Satyamandira, is now referred to as Vedabhavana in the text, in the Nārada's questionnaire to Brahmā, who asked as to what Rāma did after establishing Vedabhavana. In answer, he was told that Brahmanas ruled the forest.

There seems to be some kind of overlapping in the beginning of the description, in the text, for this period. The previous settlement of Satyamandira appears to have been confused with Vedabhavana, in the narration of the accounts[17]. Inspired by the merits of visits to Harikṣetra and Suvarṇā, Rāma is said to have undertaken the second journey to that religious centre. The eighteen Mehi-Vāḍava Trivedis (*traividya*) – Kuśika, Kauśika, Vatsa, Upamanyu, Kaśyapa, Kṛṣṇa, Ātreya, Bharadvāja, Dhāriṇa, Śaunaka, Māṇḍavya, Bhārgava, Paiṅgya, Vatsya, Laugākṣa, Gāṅgāyana, Gaṅgeya, and Śunaka[18], who had been living in Dharmāraṇya ever since its establishment by the three gods, in *Tretā*, were excellent experts of the Vedas. Previously chosen (*vṛta*) by Rāma, they were again called upon to officiate as priests for the sacrifice (*yajña*) for him. They were settled as before in that Moherakapur[19]. In honour of Sīta, a city called Sītapur, with Śāntā as its tutelary deity, was established by Rāma. On this occasion twelve villages were given to the Brahmanas in the vicinity of Moherakapur. Then, he is stated to have left for pilgrimage on Kāśyapī. Some of the Vāḍavas were brought after the conclusion of the sacrifice of Dharmālaya, to a place, where Dharma did penance. Besides, sixteen great donations were given by Rāma. Fifty five villages were settled and given to the Brahmanas. These 55 villages extended up to Satyamandira. There were 24 families (*kula*) of 18,000 Brahmanas. The names of the fifty-five villages, in order are given in the first list of the consolidated names (*Appendix I*)[20]. 36,000 Vaiśyas, 1,44,000 Śūdras, cows, cloths, gold, silver, copper, grains and unlimited wealth were given to the Brahmanas. Small villages and places were also given to them. 'Who lives where, that becomes his', following this maxim, the Brahmanas seem to have enjoyed those places from Tretā to Dvāpara, and till the arrival of the Kali age. There runs the decree of Śrīmātā and the Brahmanas. These places were full of the resonance of the Vedic chantings and ceremonies.

CULTURAL PERIOD IV

A. Structural Period VIII

I. *Derecognition and Forfeiture of the Landgrants of the Brahmanas*

The coming of the *Kali* age, augured well neither for the Brahmanas nor for Dharmāraṇya and its deniziens. In the long span of life, described in the area, there were three desertions, migrations, and reoccupations of the site and its occupants. The *Kali* and Āma, the King of Kanyakubja visited simultaneously on the scene. Afraid of *Kali* and unrighteousness, all the deities leaving earth, took refuge in Naimiṣāraṇya, and Rāma is stated to have gone to Setubandha with his associates.[21] Under the shadow of Indrasūri (Hemachandra?), the Kanyakubja King, turned out to become a follower of Jainism and he married his daughter, and gave Moherakapur in marriage to Kumārapāla, who came to Dharmāraṇya and made it his capital. Jainism was proclaimed state religion. He derecognised the charter of the Brahmanas and their lordships over these places, with the result that they had to run from pillar to the post. When they contacted Āma, they were told to go to Kumārapāla, who retorted them by saying, "neither of your three deities, was in Dharmāraṇya, nor Dharma existed there; Where are your benefactors, Rāma and Hanumāna? Neither, we have seen the charter, nor, I follow it. Vāḍavas! show me Māruti, recognising whom, I will do your work."

Crestfallen, Vāḍavas came back. In a congregation, they decided to reach Setubandha *en masse* for seeking the help from Rāma. 3,000 out of 18,000 proceeded, while 15,000 Brahmanas stayed back doing their daily chores. Before departure, the 3000 Vāḍavas are stated to have paid their homage to the tutelary deities (*kulamātar*), Gaṇanāyaka, who was situated in the south of that place, Bakulasvāmī, Surya, Mahāśakti, Śrīmātā, Śāntā, Jñānajā, Gotra mātā and others. After a journey of six months, they reached their destination, met Rāma's emissary, and narrated their woeful tales: how they were first established by the three deities in Dharmāraṇya; how on the decay of their places, Rāma rehabilitated them, gave 144 villages for subsistence (*vetana*), 13 other villages including Sītapur for worship (*archārtha*), 36,000 *Vaṇijas* for the service of the Brahmanas; 1,25,000 Gobhūjā, Śūdras – who became three fold – Gobhūjā, Aḍālajā and Māṇḍalīya, for subsistence (*vṛtti*) – 18,000 Moḍha, 18,000 Gobhūjās, 18,000 Māṇḍalīyas, 1,25,000 Aḍālajās, all put together.[22]

II. *Restoration of the Landgrants*

With a view to wreaking vengeance and teaching a lesson to the erring Kumārapāla, Hanumāna is said to have provided the Brahmanas with two small balls of hairs picking up from his two arms. He gave instruction to throw one of them into Kumārapāla's court. On his refusal to comply with their requests, he and his kingdom would be destroyed, and when he complied, they would throw the second ball, which would restore *status quo*. The Vāḍavas, with these instructions, were seen off to their places by seating them on a stone-slab, stretching ten *yojanas* in extent. After reaching at Anandapitha, next day, they met Kumārapāla, only to be rebuffed again, "Go to the place, where Rāma and Hanumāna are. I will not give you a single cowry (*varāṭikā*), neither village (*grāma),* nor subsistence (*vṛtti*); go, wherever you, please." The enraged *vipras* immediately employed the trick and device, as suggested by their benefactor and made Kumārapāla lay prostrate in their feet. Now, he agreed to approve the operation of the charter. The *status quo* was restored; the whole world became obedient to the Brahmanas as earlier, heretics expelled and Vaiṣṇavism restored. Out of 36,000 Gobhujā *Vaṇijas*, some of whom, had become Aḍhavīja – they were pressed into the service of the Brahmanas. They discarded Jainism and became followers of Vaiṣṇavism. The king granted the charter on the bank of the river (*Jāhnavī/Gaṅgā*) on the 13th day of the bright fortnight of Pauṣa. On the demand of a few Brahmanas, to expel those

Brahmanas, who went back from their promise and local customs, there arose a dispute on the sharing of the given subsistence (*vṛtti*). On seeing different signatures, courtiers were appointed for dispensation of justice. Thus, the number of 3000 Brahmanas, who had gone to Setubandha, became recipients of the subsistence and those who did not go there, they were done away with it, and came to be known as Chaturvidya.

As a sequel to an agreement, Brahmanas and Śūdras were brought together. Chaturvedis were settled outside the village by the King. Those, who had gone back from Rāma, but had come back again, they were known as Chaturvidyas and they were deprived of the subsistence that was granted. After the dissension, they were also barred from having any relations with the *vaṇijas*, matrimonial alliances and village subsistence (*grāma vṛtti*). They were made to settle at Sukhavasanapur. These Brahmin residents of 55 villages, were called Chaturvedis, but before that, they were Trivedis. There are 15 remote ancestors (*gotras*) of the Chaturvedis. Their place-names are narrated accordingly, in the Second Column of the Consolidated lists of the Granted Villages (*Appendix I*). The *gotras* of their places and eldest ancestors (*pravara*) are mentioned. Having known remote ancestors, eldest ancestors and their places, they became known as originating from their places (*svasthānavāsin*).[23]

There is a detailed list of the 55 villages in the text[24], with some variations, when compared with the First and Second lists. For comparison and contrast, it will be useful to see the appended Consolidated list of the 55 Villages Granted to Brahmanas (*Appendix I*).

We get the Fourth list of 35 Villages (*Appendix I*)[25], with variations in their names in the details given about the origin of their remote ancestors (*gotra*), family (*kula*), and one's original place (*svasthāna*).

There are 55 Original Places (*svasthāna*) of the Trivedis. There is also mention of Nineteen Original Places (*svasthāna*) of the Chaturvedis too, but referred to as Seventeen only, in the text: Śilā, Maṇḍorā, Evaḍī, Gundarāṇā, Kalyāṇīyā, Degāma, Nāyakapurā, Ḍalīā, Kaḍovyā, Kohāṭoyā, Haraḍīyā, Bhadukīyā, Saṁprāṇāvā, Kaṅdrāvā, Śaraṇdāvā, Lolāsaṇā and Nāgalapurā.[26]

B. Structural Period IX

I. *Changes in the Avocations of the Vāḍavas and the Śūdras*

In spite of the amicable settlements of the disputes of the Brahmanas and other people at Dharmāraṇya, peace and tranquility do not appear to have reigned supreme there. In course of time, due to the rise of differences in customs, languages and dress among the 15,000 Vāḍavas, there was a deep crisis and they took recourse to different professions, such as agriculture (*kṛṣi*), wrestling (*mallāḥ*), recitations of the Vedas (*vedapāṭhakāḥ*), practice of Āyurveda, washing of clothes (*rajaka*), officiating at sacrifices (*yājakāḥ*), meditation and ablution (*saṅdhyāsnānaparāḥ*), indigo plantation (*nīlakartṛn*), thread spinning (*tantukṛt*), begging (*yāchanaratāḥ*) and weaving (*tantuvāya*).

II. *Changes in the Social Practices of the Vāḍavas*

The Śūdras could not remain aloof from this crisis. There developed a sharp distinction among their kinsmen. They were held outcast, in so far as inter-dining or intermarrying was concerned. Similarly, there arose sharp division in the profession of the *Vaṇijas*. In the *Kali* age, they are stated to have strayed from the path. Many of them became oil-miller (*tailakāra*), metal polish workers (*kalakāra*), rice dealers (*taṅdulakāriṇah*), whereas many became dependent on the princes (*rājaputrāśritāḥ*) and some became dependent on various *varṇas* (*nānāvarṇasamāśritāḥ*). Some of them settled in Sītapur. Some settled down on the banks of Sabaramati river, and some settled here and there. Those who came terrified from Sītapur, settled in Shrikṣetra town, on the northern bank of Sabaramati, when they were provided Sukhavāsaṇapur. Again, they went on their own to Sītapur. Those deprived of subsistence, settled in the middle of Dharmāraṇya on the approval of the Chaturvedis.

The poor Chaturvedis grazed cows, not far off from Dharmāraṇya. Many of the sons of Brahmanas became cowherds. The children of Chaturvedis took to cow-grazing, providing foods, drinks and other things to the Trivedis, bringing the maidens, widows and children. After some lapse of time, there developed an affair between the cowherds and maiden Brahmins. They expected, and on knowledge, were expelled and made outcast. The children born from them, became known as maiden's sons (*kātibhā*) and widow's sons (*golakā*), i.e., a widow's bastards. They became famous by the name, Dhenujā and lived on alms.

The lepers, lames, dunce, surdimates, one-eyed, and humped ones, among the Trivedis, who were left unmarried, but by dint of having lot of money, they depended on Chaturvedis' daughters. The children born from their union became famous as born from three leaves (*tridalajā*). They enjoyed subsistence by mixing up (*miśrasmudbhavāḥ*).

So far as the collection of taxes in the granted villages was concerned, the Brahmanas used to retain half of it with them and submitted the other half only[27], after giving tribute (*bali*) to the villages. When, on the enquiry from the merchant tax collector of the village (*grāmagrāhayitā vaṇika*), the secret was revealed, the sons of the Brahmanas got offended and the eleven Brahmana disputants, who disproved of this malpractice, were expelled from their kinship (*jñāti*). This kinship (*jñāti*) of eleven became world-famous for eleven years. No marriage, or relation was entertained with those, who lived outside village for eleven years. In this way, there came up many divisions among the Moḍha Brahmanas' kinsmen and the chiefs of their clans.

As regards the callings of the Trivedis after this kin-conflict, they seem to have been occupied with giving oblation to fire (*agnihotra*) and sacrifice (*yajña*). Some put fire together (*agnisamādhāna*), others were orthodox, or followers of *Smṛtis*, *Purāṇas*, Nyāya and exponents of Veda and Vedāṅga. They followed the traditional *dharma*.

III. *The Vāḍavas, the Copper Plate Charter and the 'So-called' Rāma's Seal*

The Vāḍavas and their famous families, who pay homage to the inscription (*likhitaṁ/lekhyam*), written on an inanimate object of copper (*raktapāda*), occupy the highest place in their lineage (*jñāti śreṣṭha*). They deserve tribute (*bali*) and decoration with red sandal, saffron, and flowers. Since it was written (*likhitaṁ*) on copper, therefore, it is called *raktapāda*.

IV. *Worship of Rāma's Inscription by the Vāḍavas and Inspirations to Brahmins*

Rāma's inscription should be worshipped collectively by all. Brahmanas must always worship the sealed/stamped charter by Rāma's own hands (*rāmasya karamudrāṁ*). Whosoever err, or, are found guilty of foul play, they all should be given punishment by the Brahmanas. Brahmanas cannot adopt the mark (*chihna*) of Rāma's seal (*rāmamudrāyā*), without giving the punishment, no seal of Rāma (*mudrāchihna*) can be held. Vāḍavas, the excellent lord of men (*nṛpaśattamā*), should be recognized by the marks of Rāma's seal (*mudrāhastāḥ*).[28]

It is ordained that on the occasion of the birth of a male child, Śrīmātā should be given tribute. The Brahmanas would give half of the subsistence to the remote ancestress (*gotra devī*). Two-fold should be given by the *Vaṇijas*. For Aḍālajas, it was three-fold, whereas for the Gobhūjas, it was four-fold. Śrīmātā and Bakulasvāmī should also get their due shares. The division of shares, subsistence, and dispensation of justice, are to be done in front of Rāma's envoy, who is said to roam about amidst the Vāḍavas in eight forms.

C. Structural Period X

I. *Displacement and Straying Away of the Merchants*

In spite of these arrangements made through charter, once again the Brahmanas do not seem to have maintained harmonious equilibrium, and created congenial conditions for the development of the settlement. Rather, they are stated to have been displaced from their places (*sthānabhraṣṭāḥ*). The crisis seems to have further deepened not only due to the displacement and straying of the *Vaṇijas*, who are stated to have left for different places and countries, not lagging far behind their Brahmana counterparts. As regards the Brahmanas, they are stated to have become inclined to partiality. They enjoyed *Mlechchha* villages in league with the royal family of the Kolavidhavaṁsi. They had gone far away from the Vedas at this stage of the *Kali* age.[29]

There seems to be some kind of identity crisis for them. A question about their identification is raised in the text. The answer given is: One who is connected with whichever occupation, that becomes his mark. Anywhere, they can be distinguished only by marks (*avaṭaṅkaiḥ*), not otherwise. They can be identified by their remote ancestors (*gotra*), eldest ancestors (*pravara*) and marks (*avaṭaṅka*).[30]

NOTES

1. *Skandapurāṇa,* 3.2.2.3-25.
2. It is curious to know the exact time and identity of Lohāsura, who is stated to have brought about destruction of the site at such a large scale. But both his timing and identity remains a mystery. However, recently a text called *Lohāsura Māhātmya* has come to our notice, which may throw some light on him and his acts. One thing is clear that this demon needs historical identification.
3. *Tataste vāḍavāḥsarve lohāsurabhayāturāḥ*
   praṇaṣṭāḥ saparivārā gatāste vai diśo dasa,
   Skandapurāṇa, 3.2.24.36.
4. *Samājagmustadārājan svasvasthāne samāviśan,*
   Skandapurāṇa, 3.2.11.6. The demon Lolajihvā may be identified with the mother of Madhu demon.
5. *Ibid.* 3.2.13.
6. *Karṇāṭākhyo mahāraudro dānavo madagarvitaḥ,*
   Ibid. 3.2.18.53; and also:
   Tam dṛṣṭvā tadbhayāllokaḥ pradudrāva nirantaraṁ
   tyaktvā sthānaṁ gatāḥ sarve vaṇijo vāḍavādayaḥ,
   Ibid. 3.2.18. 2-3. With which particular historical personage this demon

Karṇatā is to be identified, remains illusive.

7. *Tatrodvignā dvijāḥ sarve palāyante diśo dasa,*
gatāḥ sarve bhūmidevāstyaktvā sthānaṁ manoramam
yatra yatra mahattīrthaṁ tatra tatra gatāḥ divjāḥ,
Ibid. 3.2.18.28.
8. *Ibid.* 3.2.32.70.
9. *Ibid.* 3.2.32.19-20.
10. *Śūnyāvarte chiram kāle yathādosāstathaiva hi,*
dharmāraṇyasya kṣetrasya viddhi māmadhidevatāṁ ||
varṣāṇi dvādasehaiva jātāni duḥkhitāsmyaham |
nirjanatvaṁ mamādya tvamuddharasva mahāmate ||
lohāsura bhayādrāma viprāḥ sarve diśo dasa |
gatāścha vaṇijāḥ sarve yathāsthānaṁ suduḥkhitā ||
sa daityo ghātito rāma devaiḥ surabhayaṅkaraḥ |
na te janāḥ samāyānti tadbhayādāti saṁkitāḥ ||
adya vai dvādaśa samāḥ śūnyāgāramanāthavat,
Ibid. 3.2.32.19-24. Monier William's *Sanskrit-English Dictionary* mentions works called *Lohāsura Māhātmya* and *Lohārṇava.* It also refers to *Lohārgala Tirtha.* vide, p. 909.
11. *Yasmāchcha dīrghikāyām me snānadānodyato janāḥ* ||
rāma tasyāṁ dīrghikāyāṁ nipataṅti cha sūkarāḥ
yatrāṅganā bhartṛyutā jalakrīḍāparāyaṇāḥ ||
chikrīḍustatra mahiṣā nipatanti jalāśaye ||
yatra sthāne supuṣpānāṁ prākarāḥ prachuro 'abhavad ||
tadruddhaṁ kaṇṭakairvṛkshaiḥ siṁhavyāghra samākulaiḥ |
saṁchikrīḍuḥ kumārāścha yasyāṁ bhūmau niraṅtaram ||
kumāryaśchitrakāṇām cha tatra krīḍaṅti harṣitāḥ ||
akurvanvāḍavā yatra vedagānaṁ nirantaram ||
śivānāṁ tatra phetkārāḥ śrūyante 'ati bhayaṅkarāḥ ||
yatra dhūmo 'agnihotrāṇāṁ dṛṣyate vai gṛhe gṛhe ||
tatra dāvāḥ sadhūmaścha dṛśyante 'atyulbaṇā bhṛśaṁ ||
nṛtyante narttakā yatra harṣitā hi dvijāgrataḥ ||
tatraiva bhūtavetāla pretāḥ nṛtyanti mohitāḥ ||
nṛpāḥ yatra sabhāyāṁ tu nyasīdanmaṅtratatparāḥ ||
tasminsthāne niṣīdanti gavayā ṛkṣaśallakāḥ ||
āvāsā yatra dṛśyaṅte dvijānāṁ vaṇijāṁ tathā ||
kuṭṭimapratimā rāma dṛṣyante'tra bilāni vai ||
koṭarāṇīh vṛkṣāṇāṁ gavākṣāṇīh sarvataḥ ||
chatuṣkā yajñavedīrhi sochhrāyāhyabhavatpurā ||
te 'atra valmīkanichayairdṛśyaṅte pariveṣṭitāḥ ||
evaṁvidhaṁ nivāsaṁ me viddhi rāma nṛpottama ||
śūnyaṁ tu sarvato yasmānnivāsāya dvijā gatāḥ ||
ten tu sumahadduḥkham tasmāttrāhi nareśvara ||
Skandapurāṇa, 3.2.32.24-36.
12. *Ibid.* 3.2.33.

13. *Ibid.* 3.2.33.16.
14. *vivāhādau sadā bhāvyaṁ chāmarairmaṅgalaṁ varaṁ* ||
    khaṅgaṁ śubhaṁ tadā dhāryyaṁ mama chihnaṁ kare sthitaṁ ||
    Ibid. 3.2.33.34.
15. *Tenedaṁ śāsanaṁ dattamakshayaṁ na kathaṁ bhavet* ||
    svavaṁśavarṇanaṁ tatra likhitvā svayameva tu ||
    deśakālādikaṁ sarvaṁ lilekha vidhipūrvakaṁ ||
    svamudrāchihnitaṁ tatra traividyebhyastathā dadau ||
    chatuśchatvāriṅśavarṣo rāmo daśarathātmajaḥ ||
    Ibid. 3.2.34.15-17.
16. The King should get the land grants recorded for the knowledge of the petty future Chiefs of men. He should cause this charter to be written either on cloths, or copper plates by marking it with seals, mentioning his lineage, the size of the granted land and warning against its discontinuance:
    Dattvā bhūmiṁ nibaṅdhaṁ vā
    kṛtvā lekhyaṁ tu kārayet
    kasmat-
    āgāmi kṣudranṛpatiparijñānāya pārthivaḥ
    paṭe vā tāmrapaṭṭe vā svamudrāparichihnitaṁ
    abhilekhyātmano vaṅsyānātmānam cha mahīpatiḥ
    pratigraha parimāṇam dānachchhedopavarṇanaṁ
    svahasta kāla saṁpannaṁ śāsanaṁ kārayet sthiraṁ
    svahasta mudrāskandhavasa samāvāsa nāma deśādichihnitaṁ
    ādau eva abhilekhanīyaḥ pūrvapuruṣastrayaḥ,
    Yājñavalkyasmṛti with the Commentary Bālakrīḍā of Viśvarūpāchārya ed. Mahamahopadhyaya T. Ganapati Sastri, Delhi, 1982, vv. 314-16.
17. *Saṁsthāpya vedabhavanaṁ vidhivaddvijasattamān* ||
    kiṁ chakre raghunāthastu bhūyo 'ayodhyāṁ gatastadā ||
    Ibid. 3.2.35.2.
18. *Ibid.* 3.2.35.19-21.
19. *Svāminpūrvaṁ tvayā viprā vṛtā ye vedapāragāḥ* ||
    brahmaviṣṇumaheśena nirmitā ye purā dvijāḥ ||
    kṛte tretāyuge chaiva dharmāraṇya nivāsinaḥ ||
    viprāṅstānvai vṛṇuṣva tvaṁ taireva sādhako 'adhvarāḥ ||
    tachchhrutvā rāmadeven āhūtā brāhmaṇāstadā ||
    sthāpitāścha yathā pūrvamasminmoherakepure ||
    taistvaṣṭādaśasaṁkhyākaistraividyairmehivāḍavaiḥ ||
    yajñaṁ chakāra vidhivattairevāyatabuddhibhiḥ ||
    Skandapurāṇa, 3.2.35.16-19.
20. *Ibid.* 3.2.35.37-43. Also see the Consolidated Chart, First List *(Appendix I).*
21. *Bhayātkaliviśeṣeṇa adharmasya bhayādibhiḥ* ||
    sarve devāḥ kṣitiṁ tyaktvā naimiṣāraṇyamāśritāḥ ||
    rāmopi setubaṅdhohi sasahāyo gato nṛpa ||
    Ibid. 3.2.35.14-15.

22. *Ibid.* 3.2.36.78-83.
23. See the Second List in the Consolidated Chart of the 55 Villages and also the *Skandapurāṇa*, 3.2.39.25-35.
24. Third List of the Consolidated Chart (*Appendix I*).
25. Fourth List in the Consolidated Chart (*Appendix I*).
26. See *Appendix III* and *Skandapurāṇa,* 3.2.39.78-82.
27. A somewhat similar arrangement of tax collection seems to have been made in Sind around 711-12 A.D. After Qasim's victory here, the merchant Brahmanas are stated to have been appointed by the Arab commander to collect revenue. Thenceforth, Brahmanas got their customary dues from the traders, *The Chachanamah, An Ancient History of Sind*, Tr. by Mirza Kalichbeg Fredunbeg, Delhi, reprint 1979, pp. 166-67.
28. *upāste yaścha likhitaṁ raktapādaistu vāḍavāḥ* ||
    jñātiśreṣṭhaḥ sa vijñeyo balirdeyastataḥ paraṁ
    raktachaṅdanaṁ prasādhyātha prasiddhaṁ svakulaṁ tathā
    kuṁkumāraktapādaistairgaṅdhapuṣpādi charchitāḥ
    saṁbhūya likhitaṁ tachcha raktapādaṁ taduchyate
    rāmasya lekhyaṁ te sarve pūjayaṅtu samāhitāḥ
    rāmasya karamudrāṁ cha pūjayaṅtu dvijāḥ sadā
    yeṣāṁ doṣāḥ sadāchāre·vyabhichārādayo yadi
    teṣāṁ daṇḍo vidheyastu ya ukto vidhivadvijaiḥ
    chihnaṁ na rāmamudrāyā yāvaddaṇḍaṁ dadāti na
    vinā daṇḍapradānena mudrāchihnaṁ na dhāryate
    mudrāhastāścha vijñeyā vāḍavā nṛpasattamā,
    Skandapurāṇa, 3.2.40.7-12.
29. *Kalau prāpte dvijāḥ sarve sthānabhraṣṭāḥ yatastataḥ*
    pakṣamutkalaṁ grahīṣyanti tathā syuḥ pakṣapātinaḥ
    bhokṣyante mlechchhagrāmān kolāvidhvaṅśibhiḥ kila
    vedabhraṣṭāścha te viprā bhaviṣyanti kalau yuge,
    Skandapurāṇa, 3.2.40.39-40; *Mārakaṇḍeya purāṇa*, 31.4f. for *Kolāvidhavaṅśin*.
30. *Jñāyate gotra saṁjñāatha kechichchaiva parākramaiḥ* ||
    yasyayasya cha yatkarma tasya tasyāvaṭaṅkakāḥ ||
    avaṭaṅkairhi jñāyaṅte nānyathā jñāyate kvachit ||
    gotraiścha pravaraiśchaiva avaṭaṅkairnṛpātmaja ||
    jñāyante hi dvijā rājanmoḍha brāhmaṇa sattamāḥ ||
    Skandapurāṇa, 3.2.40.43-45.

PART - II

3

Identificaticon of the Dharmāraṇya Sites and their Archaeology

There are numerous references to Dharmāraṇya in literary sources, but its identification by scholars do not take us to the exact site of our study. Dharmāraṇya occurs in the Vālmiki's *Rāmāyaṇa*[1], *Mahābhārata*[2], *Garuḍapurāṇa*[3], *Mārakaṇḍeya-purāṇa*[4], *Bṛhatsaṁhitā* of Varāhamihira[5] and Utpala's Commentary of *Bṛhatsaṁhitā.*[6] F.E. Pargiter[7] and N.L. Dey identify this area in Gaya district. According to Dey, this is a place situated four miles away from Bodha Gaya. It is Dharmāraṇya of the Buddhist records, visited by numerous pilgrims.[8] Some consider it to have comprised the portion of the district of Ballia and Ghazipur[9] in U.P., whereas others identified it with Moharpur, a place 14 miles away from Vindhyachala in the district of Mirzapur, U.P.[10] Still others trace it near Kota in Rajasthan.[11] But neither of these identifications fit the bill of the descriptions of 'Dharmāraṇya Māhātmya'. Two epicenters are seen in the preliminary identification of the Grant of 55 Villages of Trivedis, 19 of the Chaturvedis and 23 others appended along with these on the topographical map of India. The epicenters of these fall mainly within (i) the state of Gujarat, and (ii) Sītapur district in U.P.

Significance-wise, we take up the state of Gujarat, which was the centre stage of the developments described above and where most of the places referred to above become identifiable. After the identification of the name of the first settlement, called Dharmāraṇya, we will take up the identification of the four settlements of the same habitation, called Moherakapur in the text.

There are fairly a large number of books and articles on the settlement archaeology of different districts of Gujarat. It would be out of place to refer to all of their important details. However, as our text very extensively deals with the religious places, their landmarks, various deities, religious and secular structures, numerous professionals – such as agriculturists, priests, merchants, oil-men, cloth-makers, weavers, rice-dealers, metal polish workers and so on, it would be useful to relate the remarkable features of their material conditions, to the places of their concentrations. Gujarat witnessed the rise of some of the Harappan and pre-Harappan settlements on the rivers and coastal zones (Map No. V). Among them mention can be made of Hazira, Dwaraka, Lothal, Dholavira, Kuntasi, and other habitational sites like Prabhas Patan, Padri, Loteshvara, Nagwada (Mehsana district) which might have been closer to the present day coast of Gujarat. Most of these places were ports, when the sea-level was high. Among the other Harappan sites from Gujarat were Nageshwar, Shikarpur, Surkotada, Zekada, Rangapur and Madri. The impetus to urbanization came from the dynamics of internal as well as external trade, which might have been carried out from these sea-ports. It is thought that the process of urbanization in Gujarat started with its conquest by the Mauryas, which almost coincided with the infiltration of knowledge and use of the iron implements for various purposes. The activities of iron smelting in the past in Gujarat may be projected back from the local Loharia community, although in modern times they are not doing this job. The iron would have been of immense use for the people of Gujarat. They must have made use of various implements made from it in hunting, agriculture, household, crafts and ornaments. Keeping in view the availability of about a thousand objects of iron from the excavations in Gujarat, the reference to iron pillar (*lohayaṣṭikā*) and Lohāsura, in the text, who was responsible for compelling local inhabitants to leave the place and settle down into other areas, may not be surprising. Besides, the mention of a place called Lohāṭa in Kathiawar from where the Maitraka, Chief, Viṣṇusena issued his charter in the sixth century, may also have some connection with iron related activities. The distribution of iron implements of various descriptions have been reported from various sites in Gujarat, such as Akota, Amreli, Bharuch, Deonimori, Dhatva, Dwaraka, Nagal, Nagara, Shamlaji, Prabhas, Patan, Timberwa and Vallabhi.[12] Iron in Gujarat is said to be found in association with black and red ware in pre-NBP context. Somnath III, Nagara I and Timberva I also have yielded Iron finds.

Some recent studies based on cluster analysis of seven settlements have shown that the concentration of most of the settlements, influenced by foreign trade, religion and monetization are located in Saurashtra and North Gujarat.[13] The major trade-routes connecting the North and Southern parts of India went through this region. The primary functions of the excavated sites of Akota, Kāyāvaroha, Shamlaji and Goraj are said to be religious, but the presence of money exchange indicates a relatively rich material culture. According to this analysis, monetized economy was not so good in Early Historical Phase-I (700 BC-1st C. B.C), but there are ample archaeological indicators to it in late Historical Phase-II (1st C.A.D.-5th C. A.D.), which shows that there was foreign trade in this period attested by the presence of mediterranean amphora, seals, cameos etc.[14] (Plates on pp. 83-84). The nature of political influence is represented by the seals and inscriptions of the Western Kshatrapas, Guptas, Maitrakas and Traikūṭakas; whereas silver and copper coins of Western Kshatrapas, Guptas and Traikūṭakas are indicators of monetized influence[15].

The sites of Bharuch and Shamlaji show the influence of the defence system[16], whereas the site of Moḍhera (Moherakapur) performed multiple functions, such as those of a sea-port, pilgrimage centre, defence system and the system of immigrations. Let us, therefore, examine the site in detail.

A. Moherakapur (Moḍhera)

This place can be identified with Moḍhera, Modherpur, or Mundera village, which is 18 miles south of Patan and 24 kilometres from Chanasma in Mahesana district. Moḍhera village is built on a mound as high as 72 feet. In early historical times, it was a fair-sized town; the brick remains and occasional fragments of sculptured stones are reportedly scattered round the present hamlet.[17] It is stated that Moḍhera was a rich city in the fourth century A.D. Acharya Vardhamana Suri of Vallabhi had migrated to this place with the Jain *Saṁgha.*[18] Centuries ago, it was a flourishing town and a sea-port.[19] There existed for almost eight centuries near Moḍhera a very big reservoir of water, formed by a dam constructed across the Rupen river. The lake was named Karṇa Sagar after Karṇa Solanki, who built it. The dam was strong enough to last for about 750 years, for it gave way only in A.D. 1814. The area covered by the lake was about ten square metres.[20] In the ninth century, Moḍhera was a centre of pilgrimage.[21] Formerly it was a centre of solar worship. During the reign of Bhimadeva (A.D. 1022-63), a Sun temple was constructed[22] here. Constructions of Sun temple became famous in India from the fifth century.[23] During the twelfth century, Siddharaja Jayasimha converted this place into a fort, thus enhancing the importance of this town. A historiographical survey of a connossieur[24] shows that more than a dozen and half monographs have appeared on the art and architecture of the Sun temple of Moḍhera, but we do not see the same number of works about the archaeological treatment of this important site. Therefore, we switch over to the discussion of the archaeology of the site.

As seen above, the locality of Moḍhera occupies an extended mound consisting of remnants of earlier settlements. It stands out considerably from the otherwise flat, sandy landscape mostly overgrown with spurge. It is reported that to the west of the place is the ruined site of a big stepwell. On its north-eastern side a small pillared hall projects up on a steep built out of layered brick. About 500 metres further west lies the Sun temple in an open landscape at the river bed of Pushmāvati, a tributary of the Rupen. Although the roof of the building and the tower above the sanctuary are ruined, the harmonically balanced arrangement of the site gives the impression of an extraordinary work of art. According to Percy Brown, earthquake caused destruction of the temple in the 19th century. There was also an earthquake in 1819 in the desert of Kutch.[25] Archaeological research on the hill gave evidence of three stages of settlements, which are separated from one another by layers of ash marks. Remnants of fortification with gateways are still visible. They are built out of bricks. Punch-marked and Kshatrapa copper and silver coins have been found, which indicate the early date of the settlement.[26] On comparison, the textual accounts of the occupation of this site, exceeds by one more settlement. The deposit of layers of ash in the site corroborate the textual description. Similarly, the separation of each cultural phase substantiates the description of desertion and decadence of the site, although the ten structural periods are not substantiated. Occurrence of the figures of Ādityas and World protectors (*lokapalas*), in the niches of the panels of the temple[27] of twelve goddesses around the assembly hall[28]; of *apsaras*, Kubera, Ganeśa, Ashvin and 12 Sun Gods[29], of female deities[30] and various figures of Viṣṇu[31], may on comparison with the textual references to these deities present a picture of resemblance.

A large number of temples of goddesses exist at Moḍhera. Among the important ones are: Ambaji, Sarasvati, Bhadrakali, Ambevali Mata and Ashapuri. Another temple of great significance found from this place is that of the family goddess Modhesvari, or Matangi, who is worshipped by the Moḍha inhabitants.

I. *Demography of Moherakapur (Moḍhera)*

The Moḍha Brahmins are known as Moḍha, because they are said to be the original settlers of this site of Moḍhera.[32] The Brahmins of Gujarat are divided into several sub-castes such as Audīchya, Jharola, Moḍha, Nāgar, Rajgor, Sarasvat, Sarvaria, Shrigaud, Shrimali, Tapodhana and Vyasa. Of the Brahmanas of Gujarat more than half are of the Audīchya sub-caste (90,000). Moḍhs, Nāgars and Shrimalis are the other sub-divisions of this caste of local importance.[33]

II. *The Moḍha Brahmanas*

The Moḍha Brahmans acted as priests to the Moḍha *vaṇijas* and were divided into five sub-castes—Agiarasana, Chaturvedi, Dhinoja, Jethimal and Trivedi. Moḍha Brahmans were employed in different departments of administration also, but mainly as record keepers (*Mahākṣapaṭalika*).[34] Hemachandra, the great Jain priest and counsellor of Kumārapāla, was a Moḍha.[35]

III. *The Moḍha Vaiśyas*

Like Moḍha Brahamans, the Moḍha *Vaṇijas*, too derive their names from Moḍhera in the Chanasma *taluk* of Mahesana district. Among *Vaṇijas* of this district Disval, Deshval, Khadayal, Mewad, Moḍha, Nāgar, Oswal, Porwad, Shrimali, Umaovayad, are significant. The Moḍha *Vaṇijas* are divided into six different sub-castes and are also divided into Visa and Dasa.[36] According to Cambay stone inscription of the reign of Sāraṅgadeva, dated in S. 1352, Prāgvātas and Moḍhas are the best known among the Vaiśyas or *Vaṇijas*.[37]

IV. *Migrations of the Audīchya Brahmanas*

Evidence is also available of the Brahmana immigration into Gujarat from such distant places as Pāṭaliputra and Kannauj.[38] Audīchya Brahmanas are supposed to have been invited by the Chaulukya king Mularaja (A.D. 942-97) to aid in a sacrificial ceremony. When this was over, the King offered them money and grants of land to induce them to stay in this country.[39] Since they entered Gujarat from the North (*Udīcha*), they are called Audīchya. Generally, they are considered to have come from U.P.

V. *The Audīchya Prakāsh or Shree Sthala Māhātmya*

This text furnishes information about the Audīchya Brahmanas.[40] It is said that among the Brahmanas who settled in North India in Brahmāvarta on the north bank of Sarasvati river, are called Audīchya Brāhmana (Pañcha Draviḍa) and those, who settled on the south bank of Sarasvati river, are called *Prāchya* (Pañcha Gauḍa). Later, these two major castes were divided into ten sub-castes, viz. Kanadi, Dravid, Tailang, Maharashtra and Gurjar among the Pañcha Draviḍa, while the Kanojiya, Maithil, Adhyagaud, Sarasvat and Utkala among the Pañcha Gauḍa. These Brahmanas were gifted land by the King Mularaja (A.D. 942-997). Their sub-divisions are known from their original places of dwellings, viz. Siddhapur, Pushpadra, Bhokarvadiya, Kanodiya, Vadaviya, Ambasana, Chanasmaya, Mandaliya etc. Among the Audīchya Brahmanas, those who were invited by the King Mularaja of Patan, were divided into four major groups, viz. the Sahasra and the Tolakiya. The Sahasras are further sub-divided into Siddhapur Saṁpradāya and Sihor Saṁpradāya. In the district, they are mainly found in Siddhapur, Patan Kadi, Chanasma and Vadnagar *taluks*. Among the Audīchya Brahmanas, those who settled at Dandhar sub-division, are divided into two classes, viz. *Zini Pachhediwala* and *Jadi Pachhediwala*. The Audīchya's another group is the Vadnagar Pachedi, which consists of twenty five villages in the east of Siddhapur and Unjha and the surrounding village of Vadanagar. The Siddhapur and Sihor sects of Audīchya Sahasras are further sub-divided into twenty-one classes. Patanvado, mainly consisting of the Patan and Chanasma and some of the surrounding villages is also one of the important centres of Audīchya Brahmanas. They are engaged in priestly duties and religious teachings. The Smartis worship Shiva Śakti.[41] Other important ethnic group referred to in the text is that of the Kolas. Gujarat had a population of 10,76,322 Kolis before 1967.[42]

For practical reasons, it is not possible to give the details of a large number of sites mentioned in different lists emanating from our textual study. Some of these sites have either been explored, or excavated and some may be chronologically assigned to different times, ranging between palaeolithic period to the Early Medieval periods of Indian history. Vadgam from Khambayat *taluk* in Kheda district, Anandpur from Dholka *taluk* in Ahmedabad district, Chosala from Gadhada *taluk* in Bhavnagar district; and Hathab from Bhavnagar *taluk* of the same district, have been marked as Harappan sites[43], which have been identified in our list of the places. But the description of the building structures of the sites mentioned in the text do not conform to this antiquity.

B. Vaṭapatraka

Another site of significance talked about in the text is that of Vaṭapatraka. Vaṭapadra or Vaṭapatraka is the ancient name of modern Baroda. A twelfth century stone inscription of Chaulukya Kumārapāla from near Samela tank at Vadanagar distinctly refers to the city by the name Anandapura, which it describes in fanciful manner – "Here itself, Dharma was enjoying delight of Kali" (*Kalinā Naṅdaḥ*). He lived throughout the four ages (*Caturyuga*), therefore, wisemen gave it another name, Anandapura.[44] We are told that it was called Chamatkarapur, Arkasthali, Vṛddhanagar and Skandapur at different points of times.[45] Hiuen-Tsang also refers to this place as O-nan-to-pu-lo. In fact, the eulogy of Kumārapāla refers at least thrice to the settlement of the Nāgar Brahmanas at Anandapura, which is quite in keeping with the tradition current among the Nāgar Brahmanas, that Vaḍanagar was their ancient home. Abū'l Fazl in the *Āīn-i-Akbarī* has noted the opulence of the city, chiefly inhabited by the Brahmanas. According to A.S. Altekar, Anandapura of the fifth and the sixth centuries was the home of the Traividyas and Chaturvidya Brahmanas.[46] Abul Fazl's statement that it contained 3000 pagodas[47], may seem an exaggeration, but due to the dense Brahmanical settlements one can think of good number of shrines, which might have existed here. A.K. Forbes quotes an anachronistic legend, according to which, Kanek Sen, said to be an Ikshvaku Prince of Kośala kingdom, of which Ayodhya was the capital, wrested the dominions from a Prince of the Paramara lineage and founded Vaḍanagar in A.D. 144-45.[48] Similarly, the Baroda plate of the Rāṣtrakūṭā king, Karkarāja II, dated in Śaka era of 734, refers to the boundaries of this place. According to this inscription, the east of Vaṭapadra was Jambuvāvika, i.e. Jambuwāda, to the west Aṅkoṭaka, i.e., modern Akota; to the north, Vaghejhechchas, i.e., Vaghodia. During the 9th century, however, Baroda was only a village, for the grant of Karkarāja mentioned above, gives credit to him to have conferred the whole revenue of Vaṭapadra on the Brahmana donee. The plate itself states that it was a village, or *grāma.*[49] During the course of the next three centuries, the village seems to have developed into a town; for Merutuṅga calls it a *pura* when he mentions it as one of the places, where Kumārapāla had stopped for a while on his flight from Cambay to Broach, when pursued by Siddharaja. As Baroda is situated just on the road, Vaṭapadrapura of Merutuṅga is Baroda itself.[50]

I. *Excavations at Vaḍanagar*

Excavations at Vaḍanagar have shown that it was a flourishing city in A.D. 200-600.[51] The topmost level of habitation (A.D. 600-1000), shows a phase of decline. It is said that man was roaming here in the environs from the pre-historic age.[52] The Red polished ware have been found from the excavation at Vaḍanagar and is assigned to the first century of the Christian era.[53] Most of the Brahmana inhabitants of this place are stated to belong to the Pañcha Draviḍa group. There are twenty eight sub-castes of the Brahmanas – Audīchya, Chovis, Moḍha and Nāgar being the prominent ones.[54]

C. Shreesthal or Siddhapur

Shreesthal, or Shreekshetra of our text, may be identified with Siddhapur, situated about 15 miles further up the Sarasvati than Anahilapattana. It has come to acquire its present name during the twelfth century. Before that century, the name of the place was Shreesthal, for an inscription of Mularaja mentions Shreesthal and Rudramahālaya temple.[55] Al-Birūnī also makes a reference to this place in his diary. At present *Śrāddha* offerings are made here. The Chaulukya king, Mularaja invited several families of learned Brahmanas in U.P. to come to settle down in Shreesthal. The Audīchyas, Gauḍas and Kanoja still ascribe their arrival in Gujarat to the royal invitation of Mularaja given to their ancestors.[56] Siddharaja Jayasiṁha is also credited to have assigned in gift a hundred villages to Audīchya colony in the 12th century.[57]

D. Some Sites from the Panchamahals District

The Panchamahals district, which incorporates some of the important sites of our interest, such as Halol, Delol, and Godhra is the repository of rich haul of ancient cultures. V.H. Sonavane has brought to light several sites ranging from lower palaeolithic to early historic sites from different places.[58] Champaner, situated in Halol *taluk* of Panchmahals district, shows the antiquity of the site.[59] Similarly, Godhra is an ancient settlement. There is a vast tank in modern Godhra. It is considered a place of pligrimage for the Vaiṣṇavites. It is mentioned as the place of encampment, from which Śilāditya issued a grant dated in Gupta era 441.[60]

E. Kheḍabrahma

Another important site from our point of view is that of Kheḍabrahma, located in the *taluk* of the same name in Sabarkantha district. Situated on the confluence of Harnav, the Kosambi and Pakṣendranath, this has been a very important centre of pilgrimage. Shrines of Brahma, Mataji, Amba and Hiraṇyākṣi are located here. It seems that the river Suvarṇā of our text is this one. The Hiraṇyākṣi temple belongs to the 12th century.[61] It has a big idol of Brahma about 6½ feet high. There is a step well known as Brahmaji's *vav,* believed to have been built in the fourteenth century. Momin had discovered from this place some sculptures of Viṣṇu. Of these a broken image with only the head, mace and *chakra* in the hand belongs to the 7th century. Three other standing figures of Viṣṇu are variously dated.[62]

F. Dabhoi

The worship of Hayagrīva (horse-necked) form of Viṣṇu is attested by a figure of Vaikuṇṭha with Hayagrīva face found from Dabhoi, carved on the right side of the architrave on the Baroda gate.[63] Karvan from Dabhoi *taluk* is another important place of historical interest. This place was previously known as Ichchhapuri, Mayapuri, Kanabhadra, Medhavati and Kavyaroh. According to the *Karvan Māhātmya,* there was a

Brahmeśvara, a Brahmakuṇḍa, 84 Siddhis, 8 Bhairavas, 11 Mahadevas, 12 Suryas, 6 Ganapatis, 24 Goddesses and a spot of Viṣṇu.[64]

G. Viñjhan

Situated in Kutch district, the site of Viñjhan was previously 3 kms. West of its present location and was called Kanchiba Pattana in the time of Gadhe Singh. The only traces of this site are ruins of a small shrine of Kalika Mata, a shallow pool and the remains of a fortress. The Halas shifted this place to its present site. Gadhaiya coins have been found from this site.[65]

H. Mātar

Mātar, or Matṛ is another site referred to as the name and headquarters of a sub-division in the Samangadha grant of the Rāṣtrakūṭa king, Dantidurga and the tradition based on the verse of the grant asserts that the sub-division was so named because in every village thereof a grant to Brahmanas was made by the mother of the king, Dantidurga.[66]

Tracing the history of the shrines, H.D. Sankalia held that first temples in Gujarat were those of Surya and Śiva and then came the temples of Viṣṇu and following them, the temples of mother goddesses. Some bronze images of the deities have been found.[67] The prevalence of the worship of Hanumāna is associated with the Hanumana Dhado mound, one of the three mound excavated by R.N. Mehta in his Nāgara excavation and a temple built by Khanderao Gaekwad in Vadodara.[68] The Girnar Jain inscription of Vikrama Saṁvat 1288 (A.D. 1230) refers to the renovation (*tīrthoddhāra*) of many pilgrimage centres, like Dudheshvara Mahadeva temple in Dadhichipura.[69] Another important reference to be noted in the accounts of the text of *Dharmāraṇya Māhātmya* is the mention of the deity of waste land (*Śūnya Svāmī*), a deity, who was not much in limelight before.

NOTES

1. Where, Amūrtarajas, the son of Kuśa, is stated to have settled an excellent city called Dharmāraṇya:
   Amūrtarajaso nāma dharmāraṇyam mahāmatiḥ |
   chakre puravaraiḥ rājā vasunāma girivrajam ||
   Shrimadvālmīkīya Rāmāyaṇa, I (Geeta Press, Gorakhpur edition), 1.32.7.
2. The Vanaparva refers to Brahmasarovara, whose beauty excelled by Dharmāraṇya. Dharmāraṇya is said to be famous for being a place of ancestor worship:
   Tato brahmasaro gatvā dharmāraṇyopaśobhitam |
   brahmalokamavāpnoti prabhātamevaśarvarīm ||
   Vanaparva, 84-85 and
   tataḥ brahmasaro gatvā dharmāraṇyopaśobhitam
   puṇḍarīkamavāpnoti upaspṛṣya naraḥ śuchiḥ,
   Anuśāsana parva, 26.58.
3. *Chapter 83*, quoted in N.L. Dey's *The Geographical Dictionary of Ancient and Medieval India,* p. 56, Part-II, (Second Edition), London, 1927.
4. Quoted by D.C. Sircar in *Cosmography and Geography in Early Indian Literature*, p. 91, Calcutta, 1967.
5. *Ibid.*
6. *Ibid.*
7. F.E. Pargiter, *Ancient Indian Historical Traditions*, p. 264.
8. N.L. Dey, *The Geographical Dictionary of Ancient and Medieval India,* p. 56.
9. *Dr. Fuhrer and Archaeological Survey Report*, XXII, quoted by N.L. Dey.
10. D.C. Sircar, "Āma King of Kānyakubja", *Bhāratīya Vidyā*, Vol. VI (1945), fn. 3, p. 237.
11. N.L. Dey, *op. cit.,* p. 56.
12. A. Patel, "Iron From Early Historic Gujarat: A Technological Perspective", *Man and Environment, XXVIII* (1), pp. 9-10, 2003.
13. K.P. Khandwalla,"Evolution of Settlement Types, Material Culture, and Urbanism in Early Historic Period: Phase II Gujarat, Western India", *Man and Environment, XXVII (2)*, pp. 75, 77, 2002.
14. *Ibid.* p. 70.
15. *Ibid.* p. 77.
16. *Ibid.* p. 78.
17. A.S. Altekar, "Ancient Towns and Cities in Gujarat", *Indian Antiquary, 54,* p. 37 (1925).
18. H.D. Sankalia, *Prehistoric and Historic Archaeology of Gujarat,* p. 182, Delhi, 1987.
19. *Gazetteer of India, Gujarat State, Mahesana Distirct,* p. 807, Ahmedabad,1975.
20. *Indian Antiquary*, 1925, p. 37 and also see R.E. Enthoven, *Castes and Tribes of Gujarat*, I, pp. 70-71, where he gives a date of the eleventh century to the Moḍhera *kuṇḍa*, and calls it as Rāma *kuṇḍa*.
21. *Gazetteer of India, Gujarat State, Mahesana District,* p. 807.
22. *Ibid.*

23. *Indian Antiquary*, p. 37, 1925.
24. Wibke Lobo, *The Sun-Temple at Moḍhera (A Monograph on Architecture and Iconography), Band 2*, Munchen, 1982 gives a chronological list of art critiques, who either made survey of the site, or wrote on some aspects of this monument. Among these mention may be made of Colonel Monier Williams, who visited the place in 1809 as Surveyor General, A.K. Forbes (1887), James Burgess and H. Cousens in (1903). S.Bharucha, K.V. Soundarrajan, M.A. Dhaky, E.B. Havell, Stella Kramrisch, Benjamin Rowland, Percy Brown, K. Fishcher, K.F. Sompura, H. Hertel, M. Bussagh, O. Viennot and others have studied from various angles the art and architecture of this temple.
25. *Ibid.*
26. S.R. Rao, "Recent Explorations in Gujarat and Kathiawad", *Proceedings and Transactions of the All India Oriental Conference,* Seventeenth session, Ahmedabad, October-November 1953. See also Wibke Lobo, *The Sun-Temple at Moḍhera*, pp. 1-2.
27. Wibke Lobo, *The Sun-Temple at Moḍhera*, p. 59.
28. *Ibid.* p. 61.
29. *Ibid.* p. 63.
30. *Ibid.* p. 95.
31. *Ibid.* p. 102.
32. *Gazetteer of India*, *Gujarat State, Mahesana District,* pp. 807 and 834.
33. *The Imperial Gazetteer of India*, Vol. XV (*Karachi to Kottayam*), p. 177, Indian Reprint, New Edition, Faridabad.
34. H.D. Sankalia quotes *Indian Archaeology*, XI, p. 73. See *Archaeology of Gujarat* (*Including Kathiawar*), p. 208, Bombay, 1941.
35. Merutuṅga, *Prabandha Chintāmaṇi*, p. 127, quoted by Sankalia, *Ibid.*
36. *Gazetteer of India, Gujarat State, Mahesana District,* pp. 179-81.
37. H.D. Sankalia, *Archaeology of Gujarat* (*Including Kathiawar*), p. 208.
38. *Ibid.* p. 206.
39. *The Imperial Gazetteer of India*, Vol. XV (*Karachi to Kottayam*), p. 179, Indian Reprint, New Edition, Faridabad.
40. *Audichya Brahmana Annexure* I, A Note Based on *Audichya Prakash* or *Shreesthal Mahātmya* in the *Gazetteer of India, Gujarat State, Mahesana District*, p. 849.
41. *Ibid.*
42. K.M. Munshi, *Gujarat and Its Literature,* Bombay, 1967. His map shows the distribution of the Koli population.
43. H.D. Sankalia, *Prehistoric and Historic Archaeology* of *Gujarat*, pp. 187-88, Delhi, 1987.
44. *Epigraphia Indica*, I, v. 20, p. 299.
45. *Gazetteer of India, Gujarat State, Mahesana District*, p. 840.
46. *Indian Antiquary*, 1925, p. 15.
47. *Ibid.* p. 16.

48. A.K. Forbes, *Rāsa Mālā* or *Hindu Annals of the Province of Gujarat in Western India*, Delhi, 1973, *BK.I, Chapter I* quoted in the *Gujarat State District Gazetteers, Mahesana District,* p. 840 and A.S. Altekar, *op. cit.,* p. 16.
49. A.S. Altekar, *op. cit.,* p. 37.
50. *Ibid.*
51. *Indian Archaeology Review*, 1953-54, p. 10 cited in R.S. Sharma's *Urban Decay in India (C. 300-C. 1000)*, p. 74, New Delhi, 1987. Also see B. Subbarao and R.N. Mehta, "Excavations at Vadanagar", *Journal of the M.S. University of Baroda*, Vol. IV, No. 1, p. 21ff.
52. *Gazetteer of Mahesana District*, p.1.
53. R.N. Mehta, *Excavations at Shamlaji,* p. 6, Baroda, 1967.
54. *Gazetteer of India, Gujarat State, Mahesana District*, p.1.
55. A.S. Altekar, *op. cit.,* p. 44.
56. *Ibid.*
57. *Ibid.* p. 45.
58. H.D. Sankalia, *Prehistoric and Historic Archaeology of Gujarat*, p. 179.
59. R.N. Mehta, *Excavation Report at Champaner.*
60. A.S. Altekar, *op. cit.,* p. 22.
61. *Gazetteer of India, Gujarat State, Sabarkantha District*, pp. 231 and 720-21.
62. H.D. Sankalia, *op. cit.,* p. 181.
63. *Ibid.*
64. *Gazetteer of India, Gujarat State, Ahmedabad District*, p. 808.
65. *Gazetteer of India, Gujarat State, Kutch District*, p. 622 and D.P. Khakhar, *Report on the Architecture and Archaeological Remains in the Provinces of Kachh*, p. 45, Bombay, 1978.
66. A.S. Altekar, *op. cit.,* p. 36.
67. H.D. Sankalia, *Prehistoric and Historic Archaeology of Gujarat,* p. 175.
68. *Gazetteer of India, Gujarat State, Ahmedabad District,* p. 885.
69. *Indian Antiquary,* 1925, p. 24.

4
Conclusion

It would appear from the brief analytical survey of the sites made by us that some of the accounts of the puranic descriptions of *Dharmāraṇya,* its settlements, immigration and rehabilitations of the Moḍha Brahmanas,Vaiśyas and Śūdras match the archaeology of the land. In the same way, some structures and places of worship are also corroborated, when matched with it. One can easily detect the tendency among most of the ancient pilgrimage centres that they concentrate multitude of other *tīrthas* from far off places at one centre. For example, the two Vaiṣṇavite centres – Dvārāvatī *tīrtha* and Harikṣetra are said to have found locations of their places in Moheraka Kṣetra[1]; Dharmakṣetra and Shivakṣetra, described in the *Purāṇa* are to be located in this very area or, are far away from Moḍhera, cannot be said with certainty, but description-wise they show the propensity of their locations in different directions of Gujarat.

Instances in Indian history are not wanting, when some Kings by virtue of their emulating the virtues and characters of Rāma, or resemblance of their ideals with those of him, have been compared with Rāma. Sometimes, they have themselves arrogated to become Rāma, or at times were made to arrogate as Rāma. In the present context, time and situation, one may be reminded of the charitable acts of the Chaulukya King Mularaja of A.D. 942-97, of Jayasimha Siddharaja of A.D. 1094-1143, who are known to have invited large number of Brahmanas and settled them in the areas like Vadanagar, Anandapur and Siddhapur. But there is not the slightest hint either of their names, or of the philanthropic activities of these personages in anyway reflected in the description of the *Purāṇa*. Hence these cannot be linked with them. But, then how one should take the graphic descriptions of such events? Similarly, the enumerated dreadful demons, such as Jṛṁbhaka, Lohāsura, Lolajihvā, Karṇāṭa, Kolavidhvansin and the unspecified Mlechchhas, who have been held responsible for displacement and destruction of the sites, unless correctly dated and identified cannot establish the status and nature of the site in proper perspective.

As regards the whole account and anecdotes of the gift of the villages in two rounds by Rāma to the Trivedi Brahmanas by putting his signature on the copper plate charter and the Brahmanas' claim to have enjoyed these villages on the strength of the said charter ever since their occupation of the site in ancient times, obviously seems to be a collective attempt of the hapless Brahmanas to escape from the eviction of their land holdings which took place under the regime of Kumārapāla, who was more inclined to Jainism than to Brahmanism or Vaiṣṇavism. Besides seeking refuge under the shadow of the fanciful divine charter, the dispossessed Brahmanas have not only tried to assert the efficacy of their religious persuasion and saviour, Lord Rāma, who is made to appear in the 12th century to rehabilitate them and cow down the persecutors and adversaries of his devotees through his protege Hanumāna, but also tried to re-emphasize rights over the villages. This appears to be a genuine explanation of this narrative of the *Purāṇa*, but how to disentangle, reconcile and explain the frequent swearing in by the name of Rāma in most of the imprecatory verses of the land grants recorded on the copper plate charters, where the charters extolling the merits of land grants are making appeals to the current and future Kings, on behalf of Rāmchandra/ Rāmabhadra/Rāma to protect the granted lands at all costs[2]; those not doing so are threatened to fall into the hell. Needless to say that the charters recording the appeals issued in the names of Rāma/Rāmachandra/Rāmabhadra are relatively of much anterior dates (say from the 7th century) than the date of the writing of this narrative. It seems that the attempts to ensure the protection of the granted land till perpetuity in most of the charters by the reminder of Rāma's appeal and the Brahmanas' bringing in Rāma for the legitimation of the granted villages in the description of Dharmāraṇya, may have some interlinks and needs further attempts at explanation. Why the numerous land grants in their charters are very frequently appealing and cautioning the current and future Kings to harken to the appeals of Rāma and Rāmabhadra not to dispossess the Brahmanas of their precious land grants? It seems plausible to conclude that it is because of the unstable, ephemeral and transitory nature of the rulers' hold over their kingdoms that the name of a deity and the threats to suffer the consequences of forfeiture have been used by the donor of the grants.

NOTES

1. Haripriya Rangarajan, *Spread of Vaiṣṇavism in Gujarat up to 1600 A.D.*, Bombay, 1940.
2. (a) *Sarvānetān bhāvinaḥ pārthivendrān* |
   bhūyo bhūyaḥ prārthayatyeṣā rāmaḥ ||

   (b) *Sāmānyo 'yam dharmmaseturnṛpāṇāṁ* |
   kāle kāle pālanīyo bhavadbhiḥ ||
   sarvān etān bhāvinaḥ pārthivendrān |
   bhūyo bhūyo yāchate rāmabhadraḥ ||

   At some places Rām Chandra, or Rāma are used in place of Rāmabhadra in the charters.

Appendices

APPENDIX I

Consolidated List of Common Names of the 55 Villages Granted to Brahmanas, Mentioned at Four Different Places in the *Skandapurāṇa* in Context of the Narration of their Places, *Gotras*, *Pravaras* and *Gotradevis*.

(Reshuffling in order done by us for the sake of comparison)

First List Places of the Brahmanas	Second List Their *Gotras* (Remote ancestors)	Third List *Pravaras* (Eldest eminent ancestors)	Fourth List *Gotra Devis* (Female deity of the family)
(*Skandapurāṇa* 3.2.35.37-43)	(*Skandapurāṇa* 3.2.39.21-35)	(*Skandapurāṇa* 3.2.39.54-82)	(*Skandapurāṇa* 3.2.39.37-53)
Sitapur	Sitapur	Shītavāḍiyā	Sitapur
Shrīkṣetra	Shrīkṣetra	Shrīkṣetra	Shrīkṣetra
Jyeṣṭhalā	Jyeṣṭhalojā	Jyeṣṭhalojā	Jyeṣṭhalā
Shreyasthāna	Sheraṭhā	Sheraṭhāgrāma	Shreyasthāna
Daṁtālī	Tālī	Daṁtālīya	Daṁtālī
Dehaṁlohaṁ	Deholo	Dehaloḍīa	Dahloḍa/Deholoḍī
Thala	Thalagrāma	Thalagrāma	
Kohech	Kohech	Kohē	
Chandanakshetra	Chaṁdana	Chāṁdaṇakheḍe	
Hastinapur	Hāthañjam	Hāthījaṇe	
Karpaṭa	Kapaḍvāṇkam	Kapaḍvānaj	
Vanoḍa	Vanoḍī	Vanoḍīyā	
Thalatyajam	Thalajā	Thalatyajā	Thalatyajā
Chāraṇasiddhaṁ	Chāraṇaṁ/ Chāraṇīya		Charaṇīyā
Godharaṁ	Godharī	Godharīyā	
Mātrā/Mātaram	Mātrā	Mātrā	
Balavatī	Valolā/Dṛṇa	Valolā	
Gandhavatī	Sauhāsīya	Sohāsīyapuram	
Rūpāvalī	Rūpolā	Rūpolā	

(*contd.*)

First List Places of the Brahmanas	Second List Their *Gotras* (Remote ancestors)	Third List *Pravaras* (Eldest eminent ancestors)	Fourth List *Gotra Devis* (Female deity of the family)
Bahudhanaṁ	Bodhaṇī	Bodhaṇī	
Chhatritaṁ	Chatroṭā	Chatroṭā	
Vaṁśajaṁ	Vāsataḍī	Vāsaṁtaḍyāṁ	Vānsḍīā
Gotikī	Gotīyā	Gotīyānām	
Dugdhāvalī	Dudhīyā	Dudhīyā	Dudhīā
Vaihola	Vaiholā	Vaihāla	Vailola
Nālāvalī	Nālāḍā	Nālolā	Nālolā
Āsāvalī	Asālā	Asālā	Asālā
Vaṭamālikā	Maliā	Vaṭastrahāle	
Mohodhaṁ	Mahovī	Mahovīā	Mohovī
Mudgalī	Magoḍī	Magoḍoā	Mudgala
Vaṭapadraka		Vaḍodrīyā	Vaṭasthāna
Rajñaḥpur			Rajñaḥpur
Krishṇavāṭa/ Goviṅdāṇaṁ	Vrajanhorī	Goviṅdāṇā	Krishnavāṭa
Chāraṇasiddhaṁ	Chāraṇasiddhā	Vāraṇasiddhā	Nāraṇasiddhā
Phanaphāvalī	Kaṇṭāchosali	Kaṇṭavāḍīā	
Kaṅnajanhvī	Sānadīyā	Sānadā	
Shamohoralī		Shīholīyagrāma	Shīholī/Shoholī
Bhājyajaṁ	Bhālaja	Bhālajā	Bhālajā
Māraṇajaṁ	Māṇajā	Māṇajā	
Īā(mlī)	Āīyā	Īyā	Īā(Shliā)
Rājyajam	Raṅtyajā	Rājyajā	
Jāyāsaṁraṇaṁ	Jaṣāsaṇā	Jākhāṣaṇaṁ	
Chitralekhaṁ			
Chanasthanam		Krīṇavāchanas-thāna	
Haṁsāvalī	Hālola	Hāsolāsaṁ	
Chaillajam			
Suhālī	Suhālī		Suhālīyā
(K)āmataḥ	Āmataḥ		
	Nātamorā	Natamora	
	Gaṁbhīdhaṇīā	Gaṁbhīdhāṇiya	Gamīdhānīyam
	Ṭīkolīya	Ṭikolīyā	
	Pāṭadīâ	Pāṭaḍīyā	Pāṭaḍīā
	Ānaṅdīyā	Ānaṅdīyā	Ānaṅdīyā
	Saṁhāliyā	Saṁhāliyā	
		Dehola	Delola
			Sohāsīya
	Charaṇīya		Charaṇīā

(*contd.*)

First List Places of the Brahmanas	**Second List Their *Gotras* (Remote ancestors)**	**Third List *Pravaras* (Eldest eminent ancestors)**	**Fourth List *Gotra Devis* (Female deity of the family)**
Mushalī	Chhede	Khalaevatra/ Godaṇīya	Chekhalī
	Alueva/ Goladṛṇa		Golandrna
		Moūtrīyā	
	Vrajanhori	Janhorī	
		Tiyā(shrī)	Shliā
	Govyandali		
Sodgītra			
	Phīṇāva		
		Varalīyā	
			Chānchódakhe
			Koṇāyā
			Sonnanaṇḍilya
			Vailola
			Dharaṇa
			Nālola

APPENDIX II

Identification of the Names of Villages with Variations, Found at Different Places in the *Skandapurāṇa*

First List	Second List	Third List	Fourth List
Sitapur (Ahmedabad/ Sitavada in Sabarkantha/eight miles away from Modheraka in Mahesana district, *Gujarat State District Gazetteers, Mahesana*, p. 807)	Sitapur	Shitavadiya	Sitapur
Shrikṣetra (Sristhalam in *Mahesana district Gazetteer,* p. 829/ Sridharpur in E.B. Joshi's *Uttar Pradesh District Gazetteer, Sitapur*, Lucknow, 1964, pp. 318-23)	Shrīkṣetra	Shrikṣetra	Shrikṣetra
Mushali	Magoḍī (in Ilol *taluk* of *Sabarkantha District, Gujarat State District Gazetteer,* p. 129.)	Magoda	Mudgala
Mudgali	Jyeṣṭhaloja	Shiholiya-gramam (Shihora in *Vadodara District Gazetteer* map)	Shoholi (Saholi in Sitapur, U.P., H.R. Nevil, *Sitapur A Gazetteer, Vol. XI, District Gazetteers of the United Provinces of Agra and Oudh,* Lucknow, 1923, p. 323)

(*contd.*)

First List	Second List	Third List	Fourth List
Jyeṣṭhalā Shreyasthana	Sherathā Chhede	Jesthaloja Sheratha-gram	Jyesthala Shreyasthana
Dantali (Danta, in Gujarat)	Tālī	Dantaliya (Datauli in Lucknow, *District Gazetteer*, p. 26; Datlidooj festival held here)	Dantali
Vaṭapatraka (Vadnagar in Mahesana; Vadgam in Banaskantha district)	Vanoḍī	Vadodriya	Vatasthana
Rajñaḥpur *(Mahesana District Gazetteer*, p. 829/Also in Rajkot)	Govyaṁdalī	Godaniya	Rajñaḥpuram (Rajapur in Laharpur, Sitapur, U.P. see Nevil's map)
Krishnavata Deham/Loham (Dethali in Mahesana/ Dehemai in Sabarkantha)	Kaṇṭāchoshalī Kohechaṁ	Kanṭavāḍīā Vekhaloya	Krishnavata Dahloda
Chanasthanam	Chaṁdana	Chandana-khede	Chekhalī
Kohech	Sohaṁ	Thalagrāma Moutriya	Chāñchodakhe
Chandanakṣetra (Ancient name of *Vadodara, District. Gazetteer*, p.5)	Hāthaṁjam	Hathijane (Hathia, Nevil, *Sitapur, A Gazetteer*, Vol. XI, Appendix, p. XXXII)	Dehlodi Bharadvaji/ Konaya Bharadvaja/ Golamḍrṇa
Thala (Than in Rajkot)	Kapaḍvāṇakaṁ	Kapadvanaja (Kheda district)	Thalatyajā
Hastinapur Karpata	Vrajanhori Vanoḍi	Janhori Vanodiya	Naranasiddha Bhālajā

(*contd.*)

First List	Second List	Third List	Fourth List
Kannajahnvi	Viṇāṁ	Kīṇāvācha-naka	Mohovī
Vanoda (Gujarat)	Vagolaṁ	Govindana	Ia (shlia)
Phanaphavali	Dṛṇa	Thalatyaja	Anandiya
Mohodham (Mohuva in Bhavnagar)	Chāraṇamsiddhā	Varanasid-dha	Patadia
Shamohorali	Bhālajā	Bhālajā	Vansdia
Govindanam	Mahovī	Mahovia	Charaṇīā
Thalatyajam	Āīyā	Tiyashriya-math	Dudhiadharana
Charanasiddham (Sidhpur in Mahesana district)	Malia	Godhariya Vatastrahale Sanada, Manaja Anandiya	Sonnamandilya
Sodgitra	Godharī	Patadiya	Vailola
Bhajyajam	Āmataḥ	Tikoliya	Asala
Vatamalika	Suhālī	Gamidhaniya	Dharana
Godharam (Godhra district, Gujarat)	Māṇajā	Matra	Nalola
Maranajam	Sānadīyā	Natamora	Delola
Matra/Mataram (temple of Mata of Moḍhera Gujarat)	Anaṁdīyā (Anandpur, Surendra Nagar)	Valola	Sohasiya (Gandhauli in Sidhauli, Sitapur, U.P. Nevil, Vol. XI, Gandharia; E.B. Joshi, p. 323; Gandlamau, in Nevil's map of *Sitapur, A Gazetteer*)
Balavati	Pāṭadīā	Rajyaja	Suhalia (Suhai, E.B. Joshi, p. 320)
Gandhavati	Ṭikolīyā	Rupola	
Iamli (Amliyara in Sabarkantha)	Gaṁbhīdhanīā	Bodhani	

(*contd.*)

First List	Second List	Third List	Fourth List
Rajyajam	Mātrā	Chhatrota	
Rupavali	Nātamorā	Khalaevatra	
Bahudhanam (Bodhana, a place of pilgrimage in Mandavi *taluk*, Surat/Dhanpura, Dhanvada in Mahesana)	Valolā	Vasmtadyam	
	Raṅtyajā	Jakhasanam	
	Rūpolā	Gotianam	
Chatritam (Chhitiapur in Sitapur (U.P), *Āīn-i-Akbarī*)	Bodhanī (Dhan-sura, Modasa *taluka* in Sabarkanth, *District Gazetteer*, p. 711)	Varaliya (Barailia, LKO, S.D. Singh, p. 26	
Vamsajam	Chhatroṭā	Dudhiya	
Jayasamranam	Aluevā (Aluvas in Banaskanth)	Hasolasam	
Gotiki (Gotri in Vadodara)	Vāsataḍī	Vaihālā	
Chitralekham	Āmataḥ	Asālā	
Dughdhavali (Dudhai, Kutch/ Dudhala, Amreli)	Jāṣāsaṇā	Nālolā	
Hamsavali	Gotīyā	Deholaṁ	
Vaihola	Charaṇīyā	Sohāsīyā-puraṁ	
Chaillajam	Dudhīyā (in Gujarat)	Saṁhālīya	
Nalavali	Hālolā (Halol, Panch-Mahals; Irfan Habib's *Atlas of the Mughal Empire*, Delhi, 1982, p. 7A)		
Asavali	Vaiholā		
Suhali	Asālā		
(K)amatah	Nālāḍā (Irfan Habib's, *Atlas of the Mughal Empire*, Delhi, 1982, p. 7A, Nadiad)		
	Dehola (Delol, I. Habib, p. 7A).		
	Sauhāsīyā		
	Saṁhālīyā		

APPENDIX III

List of 19 Villages of the Chaturvedis (*Skandapurāṇa*, 3.2.39.78-82)

Shīlā	
Maṇḍorā	
Evaḍī	
Guṅdarāṇā	
Kalyāṇīyā	
Degama (Degrāmā)	
Nāyakapurā	(Naika in Kheda district).
Ḍalīā	(Also Dalamau in U.P.)
Kaḍovyā	
Kohāṭoyā	
Haraḍīyā	(Harad in Banaskantha, Gujarat. Also Haradia market in Sitapur, see H.R. Nevil, *Appendix*, p. XXVIV)
Bhadukīyā	(Bhadraon in Kheda distt. in Gujarat)
Saṁprāṇāvā	(Samparda in Runn of Kutch)
Kaṅdrāwā	(Kanderna and also Kandara in Irfan Habib's *Atlas of the Mughal Empire*, p. 7A; Kandaria in *Vadodara District Gazetteer* map. Also Kindhaulia in Lucknow, yielding some copper objects, cf. S.D. Singh and S.B. Singh, *The Archaeology of the Lucknow Region*, Lucknow, 1972, p.17.)
Vāsarovā	
Sharaṅḍāvā	
Lolāsaṇā	
Vārola	
Nāgalapurā	

APPENDIX IV

List of Other Place Names Occurring in the Text

Dharmāraṇya	(Dharampur, Valsad Distt., Gujarat) Also Dharampur in H.R. Nevil's, *Sitapur District Gazetteer*, Map, *Appendix*, p. XXXVIII)
Shaṁbhu-grāma	
Aḍālaja	(in Mahesana district, Gujarat, Irfan Habib's *Atlas of the Mughal Empire*, p. 7B)
Moherakpur	(Moḍhera, in Mahesana district, Moḍhera or Moḍherpur, *Mahesana District Gazetteer*, p. 807)
Sukhavāsanakpur	(Sukhsar and Vasanpur in Panchmahal district, Vasanpur in Vadodara, Sukhsar in *Panchamahals Distt. Gazetteer*, pp. 806-16, miles away from Santarampur; Sukhera in Irfan Habib's *Atlas*, p. 7A)
Satyamandira	
Moṭeraka	
Rāmeśa	
Kāmeśvara	
Māṇḍalika/ Mandal/ Mandaliya	(Mandala in *Mahesana District Gazetteer*)
Naimiṣāraṇya (Sitapur, U.P.)	
Vedabhavana	
Madhuvāsakagrāma	
Vajiṅgrāma	
Chaṇḍāla	
Dharmeshwarapur	
Moheraka/Noheraka/ Moṭeraka	
Indrastha/Indrasthāna	
Siddhasthān	(Siddhapur in Gujarat; Sidhpur also in Lucknow Sarkar, residents mostly Bais, *Āīn-i Akbarī of Abū'l Faẓl Allami* (3 vols.), Translation, H.S. Jarrett, vol.II, p.189)
Nandāpur	
Madārikā	
Dharmālaya	
Brahmāvarta	

Maps

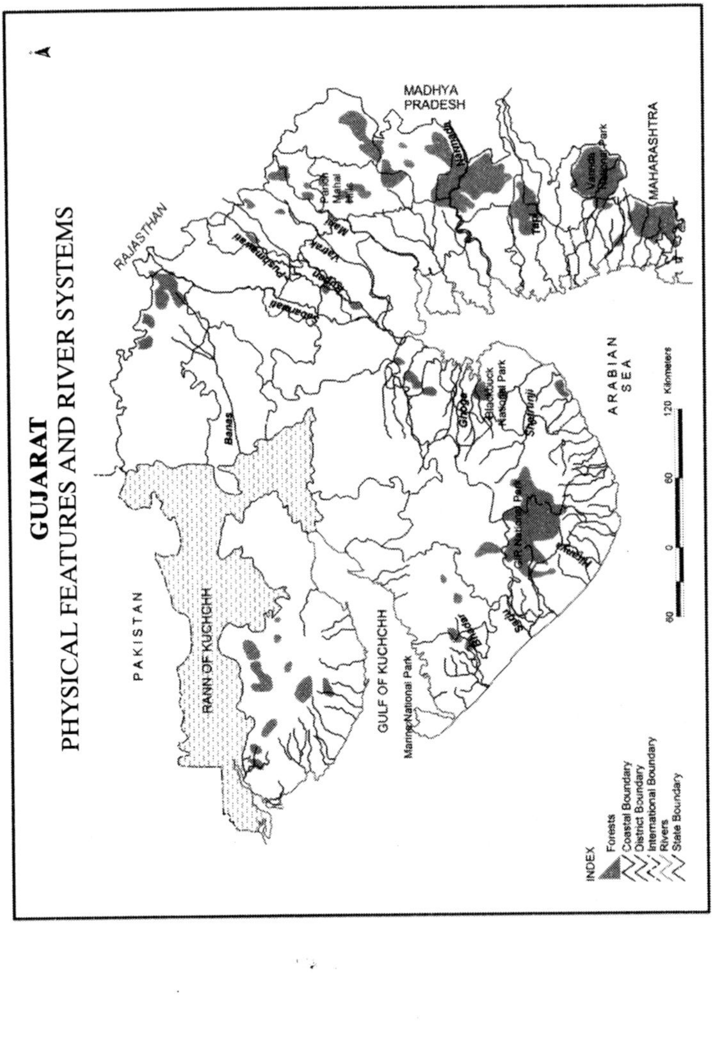

Map I

Source: Author.

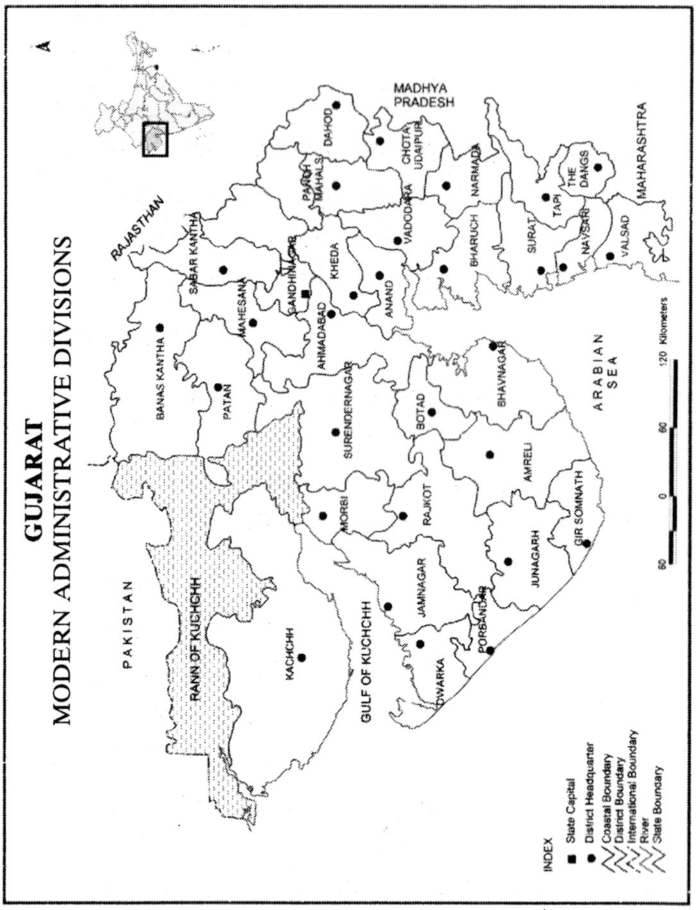

Map II

Source: Author.

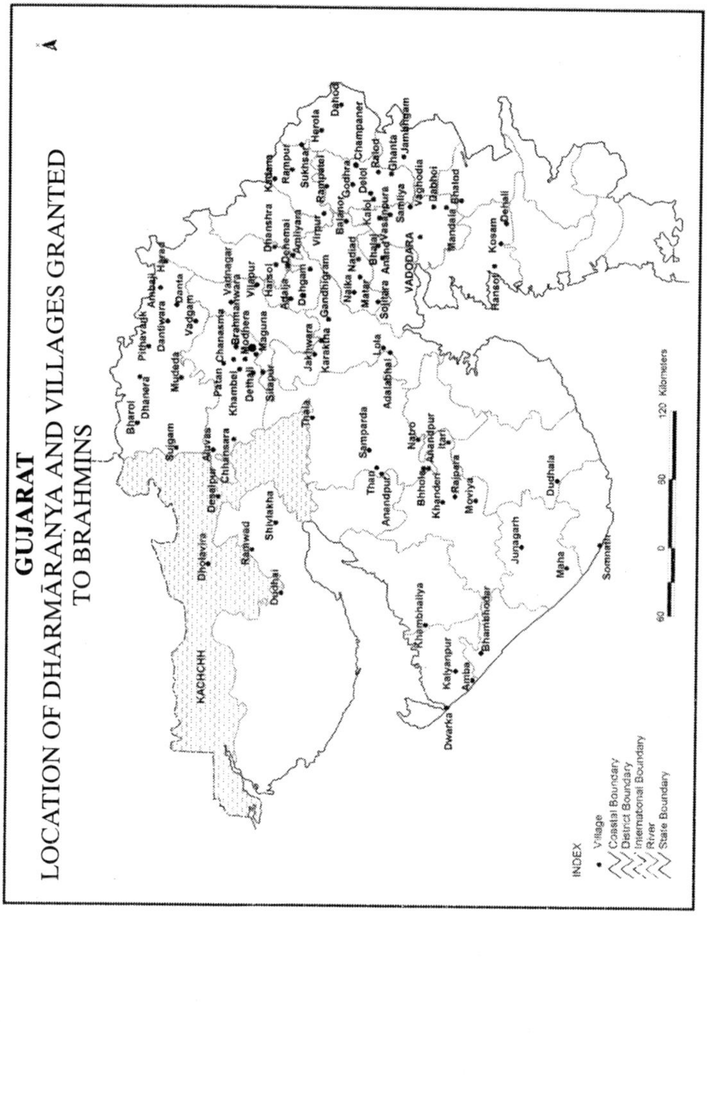

Map III

Source: Author.

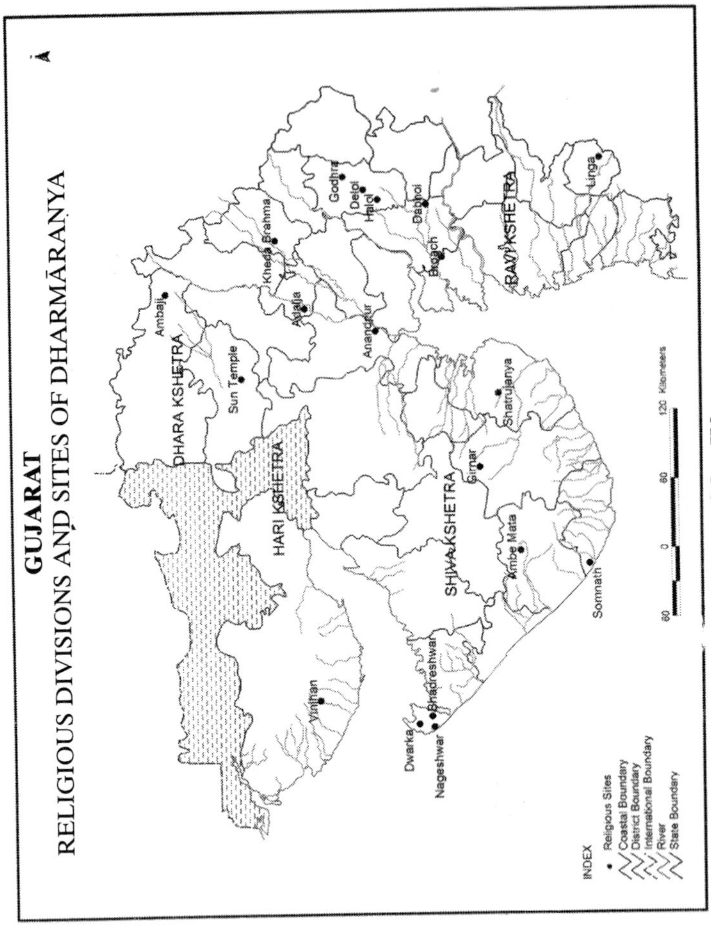

Map IV

Source: Author.

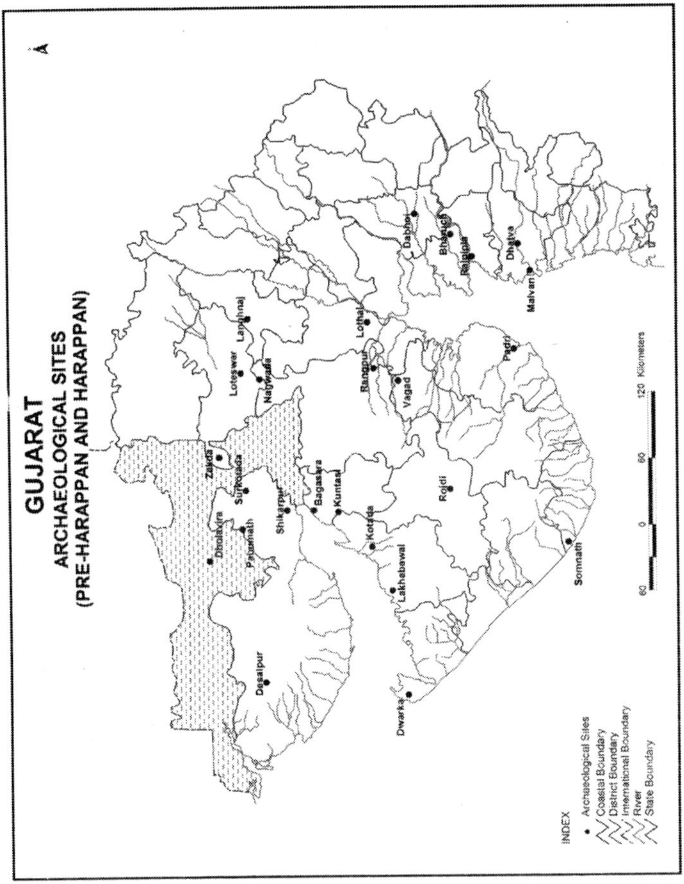

Map V

Source: Author.

Bibliography

I. Literary Sources

Primary Sources

Ain-i-Akbari of Abul Fazl Allami (3 Vols.), Translation H.S. Jarrett, Vol. II.

Audichya Brahmana Annexture I, A Note Based on *Audichya Prakash or Shreesthal Mahatmya* in the *Gazetteer of India, Gujarat State, Mahesana District.*

Mārkaṇḍeya-purāṇam (ed.) Joshi K.L. Shastri, Delhi, India, 2004.

Prabandha Chintāmaṇi of Merutuṅgācārya (ed.) Jinavijaya Muni, Shantiniketan (Bengal), 1989.

Shrimadvālmīkīya Rāmāyaṇa, I, Geeta Press, Gorakhpur edition.

*Shrī Skanda-Mahāpurāṇa:*Re-edition of Kshemaraja Shrī Kṛṣṇadāsa's edition, published from Shrī Veṅkateshvara Steam Printing Press, Bombay.

The Skanda-Mahāpurāṇam III Part : Shri Brāhmakhaṇḍa, by Nag Publishers, Delhi, 1986.

The Chachanamah, An Ancient History of Sind, Tr. by Mirza Kalichbeg Fredunbeg, Delhi, reprint 1979.

The Periplus of the Erythraean Sea, Translated from the Greek and Annotated by Wilfred H Schoff, Oriental Books Reprint Corporation, Second Edition, New Delhi-55, 1974.

Yājñavalkyasmṛti with Commentary Bālakrīḍā of Viśvarūpāchārya (ed.) Mahamahopadhyaya T. Ganapati Sastri, Delhi, 1982.

Secondary Sources

Altekar, A.S. "Ancient Towns and Cities in Gujarat", *Indian Antiquary*, 1925.

Burgess, Jas and Cousens, Henry, *The Architectural Antiquities of Northern Gujarat,* First Indian Edition, Bharatiya Publishing House, Varanasi, 1975.

Dey, N.L. *The Geographical Dictionary of Ancient and Medieval India* (Second Edition), London, 1927.

Enthoven, R.E. *Castes and Tribes of Gujarat*, I.

Forbes, A.K. *Rāsa Mālā* or *Hindu Annals of the Province of Gujarat in Western India*, BK.I, *Chapter I*, Delhi, 1973.

Gazetteer of India, Gujarat State, Mahesana Distirct, Ahmedabad, 1975.

Gazetteer of India, Gujarat State, Sabarkantha District, 1974.

Gazetteer of India, Gujarat State, Ahmedabad District, 1961.

Gazetteer of India, Gujarat State, Kutch District, 1971.

Gazetteer of India, Gujarat State, Panchmahals District.

Habib, Irfan. *Atlas of the Mughal Empire*, Delhi, 1982.

History of Humanity, Vol. IV, *From the Seventh to the Sixteenth Century*, edited by M.A. Al. Bakhit, L. Bazin, S.M. Cissoko, First published by UNESCO and Routledge in 2000.

Hunter, W.W. *The Imperial Gazetteer of India*, Vol. XV (*Karachi to Kottayam*) Indian Reprint, New Edition, Faridabad.

Joshi, E.B. *Uttar Pradesh District Gazetteer Sitapur*, Lucknow, 1964.

Khandwalla, K.P. "Evolution of Settlement Types, Material Culture and Urbanism in Early Historic Period. Phase II Gujarat, Western India", *Man and Environment*, XXVII (2), New Delhi, 2002.

Lobo, Wibke. *The Sun-Temple at Moḍhera* (*A Monograph on Architecture and Iconography*), *Band* 2, Munchen, 1982.

Nevil, H.R. *Sitapur A Gazetteer*, Vol. XI, *District Gazetteers of the United Provinces of Agra and Oudh*, Lucknow, 1923.

Pargiter, F.E. *Ancient Indian Historical Traditions.*

Patel, A. "Iron From Early Historic Gujarat: A Technological Perspective", *Man and Environment*, XXVIII (1), New Delhi, 2003.

Rangarajan, Haripriya. *Spread of Vaiṣṇavism in Gujarat up to 1600 A.D.*, Bombay, 1940.

Rapson, E.J., *Ancient India* (*From the Earliest Times to the First Century A.D.*), Delhi, 1985.

Sharma, R.S. *Urban Decay in India (C. 300-C. 1000)*, New Delhi, 1987.

Singh, S.D. and Singh, S.B. *The Archaeology of the Lucknow Region*, Lucknow, 1972.

Sircar, D.C. *Cosmography and Geography in Early Indian Literature*, Calcutta, 1967.

Sircar, D.C. "Āma King of Kanyakubja", *Bharatīya Vidyā*, Vol. VI, 1945.

Thapar, Romila, *Somanatha : The Many Voices of a History*, Penguin, 2004.

Thapar, Romila, *Asoka and the Decline of the Mauryas*, Oxford University Press, 1961.

II. Archaeological Sources

Archaeological Survey Report, XXII.

Bisht, R.S. *Excavations at Dholavira* 1989-2005, 2015.

Corpus Inscriptionum Indicarum, Vol. I, *Inscriptions of Asoka* (ed.) E. Huttzsch, reprint, Varanasi, 1969.

Corpus Inscriptionum Indicarum, Vol. III, *Inscriptions of the Early Gupta Kings* (previously edited by J.F. Fleet, but later) revised by Devadatta Ramakrishna Bhandarkar and edited by Bahadurchand Chhabra and Govind Swamirao Gai, ASI, New Delhi, 1981.

Epigraphia Indica, I, Calcutta, Delhi.

Indian Archaeology Review, New Delhi, 1953-54.

Khakhar, D.P. *Report on the Architecture and Archaeological Remains in the Provinces of Kachh*, Bombay, 1978.

Mehta, R.N. *Excavation Report at Champaner.*

Mehta, R.N. *Excavations at Shamlaji,* Baroda,1967.

Rao, S.R. "Recent Explorations in Gujarat and Kathiawad", *Proceedings and Transactions of the All India Oriental Conference,* Seventeenth session, Ahmedabad, October-November 1953.

Sankalia, H.D. *Prehistoric and Historic Archaeology of Gujarat,* Delhi, 1987.

Sankalia, H.D. *The Archaeology of Gujarat (Including Kathiawar),* First Edition, Bombay, 1941.

Sircar, D.C. *Select Inscriptions: Bearing on Indian History and Civilization,* Vol. I, Delhi, 1993.

Subbarao, B. and Mehta, R.N."Excavations at Vadanagar", *Journal of the M.S. University of Baroda*, Vol. IV, No. 1, Baroda.

Plates

Harappan Sites

1. Lothal

Source: Google.

2. Lothal Dockyard

Source: Google.

3. Dholavira: Excavated site

Source: Google.

4. Dholavira—Trench in Castle showing structural Levels

Source: R.S. Bisht, *Excavations at Dholavira 1989-2005* (2015).

Girnar Rock Edict and Some Important Inscriptions

5. Girnar (Junagadh) Rock Edict with the Ashokan rock edicts and the Inscriptions of Rudradaman and Skandagupta.

Source: E.J. Rapson, *Ancient India (From the Earliest Times to the First Century A.D.)*, 1985.

6. Girnar Rock Inscription

Source: Google.

7. Girnar

Source: Corpus Inscriptionum Indicarum, Vol. I, *Inscriptions of Ashoka*, 1961.

8. Girnar Rock Edict-I and II of Ashoka

9. Girnar Rock Edict-III and IV of Ashoka

Source: D.C. Sircar, *Select Inscriptions: Bearing on Indian History and Civilization*, Vol. I, 1993.

10. Junagadh Inscription of Rudradaman, Section-1, Left part

Source: D.C. Sircar, *Select Inscriptions: Bearing on Indian History and Civilization*, Vol. I, 1993.

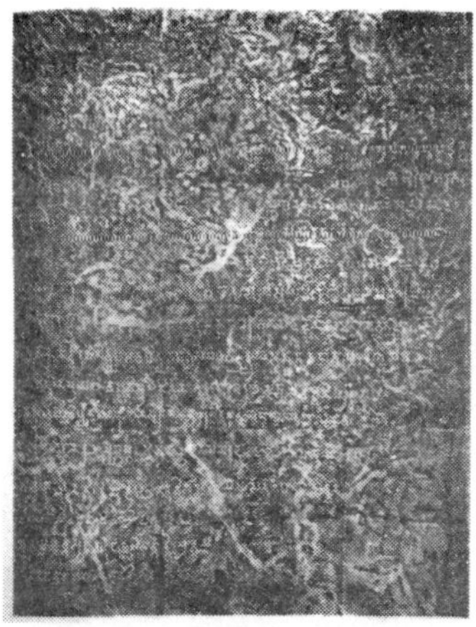

11. Junāgaḍh Inscription of Rudradaman, Section-2, Central Part

12. Junāgaḍh Inscription of Rudradaman, Section-3, Right Part

Source: D.C. Sircar, *Select Inscriptions: Bearing on Indian History and Civilization*, Vol. I, 1993.

13. Junāgaḍh Rock Inscription of Skandagupta

Source: Corpus Inscriptionum Indicarum, Vol. III (Revised) : *Inscriptions of the Early Gupta Kings*, 1981.

14. Veraval Inscription of Chaulukya - Vaghela Arjuna, 1264. A.D. It records the agreement between Nur-ud-din Firuz and the Panchakula of Somanatha relating to the building of a mosque at Somanatha

Source: Romila Thapar, *Somanatha: The Many Voices of a History.*

15. Bilingual Inscription on Mahmud Ghazni's Coin

Source: Romila Thapar, *Somanatha: The Many Voices of a History.*

Some Important Temples and Deities

16. Old Temple at Moḍhera from the south-west

Source: Jas Burgess and Henry Cousens, *The Architectural Antiquities of Northern Gujarat*, 1975.

17. Mandapa in front of the Temple at Moḍhera

Source: Jas Burgess and Henry Cousens, *The Architectural Antiquities of Northern Gujarat*, 1975.

18. Moḍhera—Open Mandapa in front of the Temple from the south-west

Source: Jas Burgess and Henry Cousens, *The Architectural Antiquities of Northern Gujarat*, 1975.

19. Surya Narayana Temple, Prabhas

Source: H.D. Sankalia, *The Archaeology of Gujarat (Including Kathiawar),* 1941.

20. The Temple of Somanatha

Source: Romila Thapar, *Somanatha: The Many Voices of a History.*

21. Brahma and Surya, Moḍhera

Source: H.D. Sankalia, *The Archaeology of Gujarat (Including Kathiawar)*, 1941.

22. Unique Image of Surya, Prabhas

Source: H.D. Sankalia, *The Archaeology of Gujarat (Including Kathiawar)*, 1941.

23. Surya

Source: Jas Burgess and Henry Cousens, *The Architectural Antiquities of Northern Gujarat*, 1975.

24. Lord Vishnu in Varaha *avatar* on Inner wall of Rani ki Vav, Patan, Gujarat

Source: Google.

25. Hayagriva Vishnu's statute

Source: Google.

26. Hayagriva Vishnu

Source: Google.

27. Hayagriva Vishnu

Source: Google.

28. Hayagriva Vishnu

Source: Google.

29. Sitalā, Moḍhera

Source: H.D. Sankalia, *The Archaeology of Gujarat (Including Kathiawar)*, 1941.

30. Deities at Somanatha

Source: Romila Thapar, *Somanatha: The Many Voices of a History.*

Connections with the World through Trade

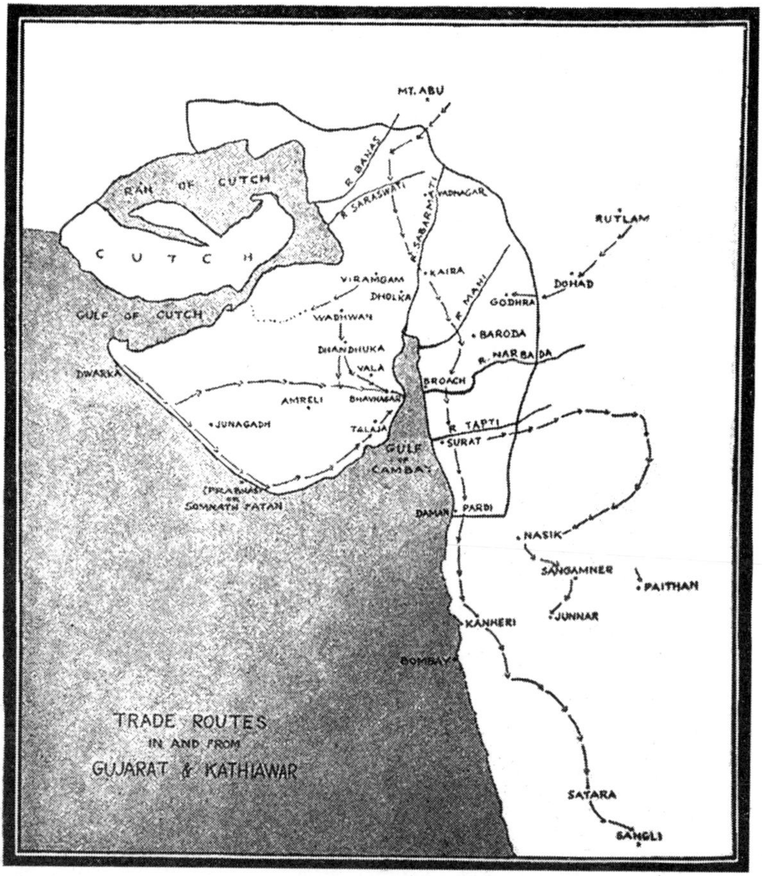

31. Trade Routes, Gujarat and Kathiawar

Source: H.D. Sankalia, *The Archaeology of Gujarat (Including Kathiawar)*, 1941.

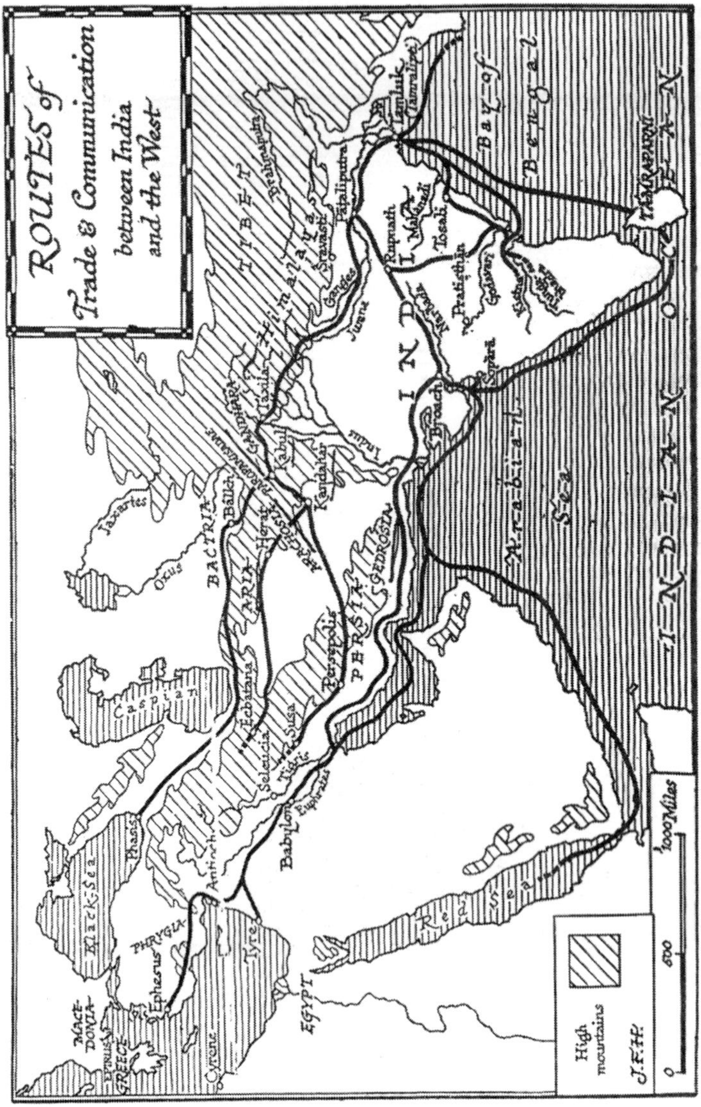

32. Routes of Trade and Communication between India and the West

Source: Romila Thapar, *Asoka and the Decline of the Mauryas.*

Ships

33. Gujarati Ship of about 600 A.D. from the Boroboedor frieze

Source: *The Periplus of the Erythraean Sea*, Transalted from the Greek and Annotated by Wilfred H. Schoff, New Delhi, Second Edition, 1974. Originally published in 1912 by Longmans Green and Company, New York.

34. Muslim Dhow as used in Indian Ocean

Source: *History of Humanity*, Vol. IV, *From the Seventh to the Sixteenth Century*, edited by M.A. Al. Bakhit, L. Bazin, S.M. Cissoko.

35. Fully Rigged Portuguese Caravela (late 15th century) launched by Iberian powers for Atlantic and Indian Ocean Conquest at the close of the 15th century

Source: History of Humanity, Vol. IV, *From the Seventh to thc Sixteenth Century*, edited by M.A. Al. Bakhit, L. Bazin, S.M. Cissoko.

Author Index

Subject Index